Unapologetically
MODERATE

bright sky press
HOUSTON, TEXAS

2365 Rice Blvd., Suite 202
Houston, Texas 77005

ISBN: 978-1-939055-89-7

10   9   8   7   6   5   4   3   2   1

Library of Congress Cataloging-in-Publication Data on file with publisher.

Editor, Fritz Lanham
Design, Marla Y. Garcia
Cover image by Gittings

Printed in Korea through Four Colour Print Group

Unapologetically
MODERATE
My Search For A Rational Center In American Politics

BILL KING

bright sky press
HOUSTON, TEXAS

TABLE OF CONTENTS

OUT OF HURRICANE'S WAY

Would the Texas Gulf Coast, like Florida, be prepared for a mass evacuation? The mayor of Kemah doesn't think so.

By WILLIAM E. KING

ON Sept. 11, 1900, J.H.W. Stele, H.S. Murray and Rabbi Cohen, all of Galveston, sent the following telegram to Gov. Joseph Sayers:

"Gov. Sayers, send military supplies fire arms animal and human food stuff danger food riots any moment. Situation horrible can't describe for god sake help us."

Two days before, a wall of seawater had inundated almost all of Galveston Island and for miles inland on the mainland. In its wake, 8,000 people were left dead, thousands more injured. The property damage was inestimable, but most of Galveston was simply gone. To put the enormity of this disaster in perspective, the attack on the World Trade Center killed less than 3,000 people, only about a third of the number lost in the 1900 hurricane.

Since Sept. 11, 2001, we have been obsessed with preventing another terror attack. Billions have been spent on homeland security, and we subject ourselves to incredible inconvenience in the name of thwarting terrorism.

But the terror that is more likely to be visited on the Houston area is a Category 4 or 5 hurricane. And the damage it will do will dwarf anything al-Qaida can pull off. However, notwithstanding the virtually meteorological certainty that the big one is going to show up someday, we spend an infinitesimal fraction on hurricane preparedness compared with what we spend on homeland security.

First, we need to understand the dimensions of the future calamity. The Texas Division of Emergency Management, or DEM, produces storm surge maps that show how far hurricanes of various strengths will push water onto the mainland. According to these projections, a Category 4-5 storm will flood virtually all of Galveston County, all of Clear Lake, the East Side to Loop 610, all of Baytown south of I-10 and about half of Brazoria County. The surge will be 20-25 feet high. That means every house in Clear Lake will have water over its roof or up to the second story. The only struc-

King is the mayor of Kemah and the managing partner of a downtown Houston law firm. He also serves on the Bay Area Transportation Partnership's Hurricane Evacuation Committee.

Please see **HURRICANE,** *Page D5*

SLOW GOING: Traffic on Highway 69 moves at a crawl as residents evacuate Beaumont in anticipation of Hurricane Lili's landfall in October 2002.

ASSOCIATED PRESS

FROM PAGE D1

ill be visible in Ke-
be the Boardwalk
and the roofs of the
restaurants. Riding
ry 4-5 storm within
rge area is simply
ble option.

does not count the
at will occur up-
the torrential rains.
3torm Claudette
inches of rain on
in 24 hours, creat-
re. When a 25-foot
lams up that water
the flood stages
come almost too
believe. Some pre-
will be under 20
at the Clear Creek

allenge is: How do
ents in the surge
arm's way? Again,
ns of the problem
sidered. The ap-
opulation of the
be flooded by a
storm is about 1
thought of trying
ore than 1 million
matter of a day or
overwhelming.
iels estimate that
more than 24
uate everyone, if
rks perfectly. Of
l not. Cars will
id run out of gas.
ic.

the models do
account the fact
ple will wait too
and find their
tes cut off. The
146 and NASA
eight feet. A Cat-
m would flood
n as many as two
storm hits. The
ario quietly dis-
any emergency
ees thousands of
ed on highways
ed in their cars.
icy managers
result in tens of
asualties; some
of 100,000. The
ese numbers are
y should know
casions, hurri-
d Pakistan have
han 100,000
recent being in
when a storm
ed more than

e who point to
id their rela-
ies as an indi-
icanes do not
mitous threat.
xamination of
ind intensities
m from a ma-

jor storm hitting a major population center. For example, Hurricane Charley, which just hit
Florida, was a Category 4 storm,
but there were only 27 casualties. However, Charley made
landfall just north of Fort My-
ers, which is a relatively low
population area. The population
of the three counties where
Charley went ashore is less than
1 million, with the brunt of the
storm hitting Charlotte County,
which has a population of only
150,000. The population of our
coastal area is about 5 million.

Similarly, Hurricane
Frances, although massive, had

played itself out and became a
Category 3 storm by the time it
hit major population centers in
Florida. I happened to be in
Florida a few days before
Frances made landfall, and it
was clear that officials there
have done a better job of prepar-
ing for a mass evacuation.

Of particular concern here
are residents who will not be
able to evacuate themselves.
One report prepared by DEM
estimated that there were 8,000
households in Galveston
County alone in which residents
did not own a car. With an average of about three persons per
household, that means there are
about 25,000 people that will
need a ride out. Based on my experiences in our area, I think
this number could be much
higher. Add to that the sick and
elderly who physically are not
up to driving themselves
through 24 hours of rush-hour
traffic, and we have a real logis-
tical nightmare.

What I find particularly dis-
heartening about this issue is
the fatalistic attitude of emergency managers. They reli-
giously preach the dangers of a
major hurricane, but we have
gone so long without a major
storm that their warnings are
now mostly falling on deaf ears,
both in the public and in our
elected leadership. As a result,
many emergency managers
have accepted that the next ma-

jor storm is going to be an
apocalyptic disaster. I recall discussing people with substance
abuse problems, and alcoholics
in particular, at one meeting
with emergency managers and
the problems that this population presents in an evacuation.
One longtime emergency manager, in response, said causti-
cally, "They'll wash up." Of
course, it did not reflect his true
feelings, but rather the sort of
gallows humor one finds in desperate situations.

However, I cannot accept
that there is nothing that can be
done. A major storm will, no
doubt, do incredible damage,
and there will be, no doubt, lives
lost. But we can act to minimize
that loss.

Specifically, the following
steps should be taken:

■ Priority should be given in
highway design and construction to maximize hurricane
evacuation routes. SH146 is a
prime example. It is virtually
worthless as an evacuation
route. However, the Texas Department of Transportation has
had a plan to expand the highway for some time. Between the
Houston-Galveston Area Council favoring other projects and
misguided opposition by some
local leaders, the project is years
behind schedule.

■ The DEM, local govern-
ments and the media should do
a hurricane-education blitz-
krieg at the beginning of each
hurricane season. We basically
have two generations that have
grown up in this area without a
major storm. The community
memory of the devastation has
faded. In addition, each year
thousands of new residents who
are ignorant to the risk move
into the area.

■ The current structure of
each county and city calling its
own evacuation is unworkable
and should be scrapped. Instead, the state should divide
the coastline into hurricane
evacuation corridors and estab-
lish a regional evacuation task

force for each corridor. These
task forces should be charged
with the responsibility and
given the authority to develop a
comprehensive plan for the
evacuation of all citizens in
harm's way, especially those
who will be unable to evacuate
themselves.

■ Once the evacuation plans
are put in place, the personnel
responsible for executing them
should test and train on those
plans with annual simulated
evacuations. These simulations
would make it more likely that
the plans would be effective and
would be another tool to raise
the public awareness of the danger involved.

■ Texas law should be
changed to authorize manda-
tory evacuations. Florida already does so. When I was in
Florida recently, the hotel management came by and informed
me that the area would probably
be evacuated the next day and
that I would be required to
leave. Allowing individuals to
stay when there is a clear and
present danger is not only dangerous for those individuals, but
also the emergency personnel
that may be put in the position
of attempting rescues.

Yes, a comprehensive plan is
going to cost money. But so does
fighting terrorism, and we seem
to have no problem finding
funding for that fight. Notwithstanding the horror and tragedy
of the attack on the World Trade
Center, it will pale in comparison to a major storm hitting our
area if we are unprepared.

Consider this passage from
the 1999 book *Issac's Storm* by
Erik Larson: "Throughout
Galveston, men and women
stepped from their homes to
find corpses at their doorsteps.
Bodies lay everywhere. One
hundred corpses hung from a
grove of salt cedars at Heards
Lane. Some had double-
puncture wounds left by snakes.
'There were so many dead,' said
Phillip Tipp, 'you would sink
into the silt onto a body at every
other step.' He had reached
Galveston aboard a small sail
boat. We kept running into so
many dead bodies that I had to
go forward with a pike and
shove the dead out of the way."

The truth is, we cannot afford to *not* have a comprehensive hurricane evacuation plan.
If readers do not believe it, they
should imagine for a moment
being trapped with their family
on a highway with vehicles lined
up as far as they can see — whi
seawater begins to seep in
their car as the storm surge r
around them.

Introduction

I came to journalism borne on a strong wind, or at least worried about one.

After earning a bachelor's degree and a law degree, both from the University of Houston, I practiced law and managed businesses for some 40 years in the Bayou City. Almost all of these professional pursuits had a substantial interface with government at one level or another. Perhaps I was drawn to them because I have had a strong interest in political science for as long as I can remember. In any event they gave me a window on how public policy works in the real world in a number of different settings.

What I found time and again is that public policy issues are frequently complex and nuanced and that for the most part policymakers are not. They are frequently driven by ideology or, even worse, some passing political passion. I saw that dynamic on steroids in the savings and loan industry collapse during the 1980s and 1990s.

My foray into the world of journalism and writing editorial essays was complete serendipity. In the mid-1990s I decided to run for public office. After a couple of false starts I was elected to the city council in Kemah, my hometown. In 2001 I became the mayor.

The next year a hurricane named Lili threatened the Texas coast. It was tracking across the Gulf of Mexico to make landfall somewhere in the Houston area. It was then that I learned that as mayor I was responsible for emergency management in the city, including its potential evacuation.

The storm was forecast to be Category 3, which would have

flooded a good portion of Kemah. While the storm seemed to be heading straight for us, forecasters believed that a cold front coming in from northwest would push it to the east into Louisiana. Nonetheless it seemed prudent to look at my town's contingency plan.

Only problem? There was none. I contacted the county and state and found they did not have much of a plan either.

As Lili churned across the Gulf, still heading straight for us, she unexpectedly mushroomed to a Category 4 storm. If she did not take the turn to the east, we were sitting ducks. Fortunately the storm did turn as forecasters had predicted and hit along a relatively sparsely populated area of the Louisiana coast.[1]

But the experience left me shaken. If Lili had not turned and weakened and instead had slammed into our area as a Category 4 storm, it would have been an unmitigated disaster. Thousands would have been killed and most of my town wiped out. I was not about to be caught in that situation again with no plan.

So I began visiting regional and state officials to try to find out if there were any plans. Basically there were not. The Texas Department of Public Safety, charged with emergency management at the state level, gave me their 30-page evacuation plan for the Houston area. I discovered my police chief had never seen it. Nor could I find anyone else who had either.

The first two pages contained some general instructions about how various law enforcement agencies were to man and direct traffic at various key intersections throughout the region. The last 28 pages were a list of those intersections and the agency assigned to them.

And that was it. There was no plan to contraflow the freeways. I was told the state had studied contraflow and concluded it would not work. That was somewhat surprising since every other state on

---

1   Hurricane Lili also unexpectedly ran across an area of cooler water just before she made landfall, which sapped much of her strength. When she finally made landfall on October 4, 2002, she was rated as only a Category 1 storm, greatly reducing the damage and loss of life she might have otherwise caused.

the Gulf Coast had an extensive contraflow plan in the event of a hurricane evacuation.

No one had given any serious thought to how nursing homes or hospitals would be evacuated. No thought had been given to those who did not have vehicles. No one had considered how people would evacuate their pets or how they might react to being told their animals had to be left behind.

All of these turned out to be tremendous problems in the disastrous Hurricane Rita evacuation just a few years later.

So I spent a good part of the next two years meeting with regional and state officials expressing my concerns. I wrote letters, proposed possible solutions, studied other states' plans and shared those with our officials. For the most part just about everyone blew me off. I was frequently accused of being the "Chicken Little" of hurricanes.

So I did what we Americans do when our government is not doing its job. I went to the press.

Not understanding much about the opinion pages of a newspaper, I drafted an essay that ran nearly 2,000 words, far longer than most papers will consider. In it I compared the risk of another September 11-type terror attack—and the money we were spending to prevent that—to the risk of a major hurricane and our almost nonexistent efforts to mitigate that risk. I titled the piece "The Other 9-11."

In August 2004 I submitted simultaneously to the *Galveston Daily News* and the *Houston Chronicle*. A few days later a junior editor from the *News* called to tell me the piece was too long and I would need to cut it down to 600 words. I was attempting to do that a couple of days later when I got a call from the *Chronicle* saying they wanted to run the piece in its entirety on Sunday, September 12. They also told me that it would be the cover of the Chronicle's Outlook section and that they would like for me to meet with the editorial board on the subject.

The week after it was published I went to the Chronicle's offices in downtown Houston. I had dealt fairly extensively with the press in my businesses and as mayor, but I had never had a formal meeting with an editorial board and was not sure quite what to expect. Entering the room was somewhat intimidating. There were about a half dozen editorial writers and a couple of reporters. Jeff Cohen, the paper's editor, presided. He began by announcing to the group that he thought my op-ed was one of the best he had ever seen and that he was really "pissed off" that a lawyer had written it.

So began what has now been nearly a decade-long friendship, mentorship and collaboration. From the beginning Jeff believed I could write and encouraged me to do so. Over the next several years, I wrote an occasional op-ed for the *Chronicle*. Eventually that evolved into a weekly, then bi-weekly, column, plus occasional unsigned editorials.

What follows is a sampling of those columns and editorials. You will see from the table of contents that I have covered many topics. Some, like the demographic sea change our generation faces, mental health, immigration, and the country's current political dysfunction, I have found particularly compelling.

Since I write for a Houston newspaper, about half the columns address state and local issues. For those of you who do not live in Houston and may not be familiar with it, it is a remarkable city, but not well understood by outsiders. Few, for example, would know that it is ethnically the most diverse city in America. And those who view this Southern city as a bastion of conservatism might be surprised to learn it elected the first openly lesbian mayor in America. It and Texas as a whole are infinitely more complex and sophisticated than the impression left by our occasionally buffoonish politics.

In choosing columns to include in this book I have tried to reflect the range of issues I have addressed over the past 10 years, with particular emphasis on matters that continue to demand our attention.

For the most part, the columns appear here as they were published. I have resisted the impulse to edit these pieces based on subsequent information or events, even though my thinking has evolved on some of these issues.

But whether writing about national, state or local issues, the theme that runs through all this work is my belief in moderation and pragmatism, both of which are desperately needed but in short supply in our current political dialogue.

America is the first post-tribal nation in the world. We are the first and only country in human history founded on ideals rather than geography or tribal affiliations. We are the harbinger of what the rest of the world will ultimately become.

Those founding ideals—personal freedom and individual rights, the rule of law, democratic government—form the overarching architecture of our country. But in their service we have generally done what was practical and realistic. At least until the last few decades.

Beginning in the 1980s, for reasons I have not been able to completely divine, we took a sharp turn away from practicality and toward ideology. The partisan divide gradually became a chasm, compromise a dirty word. Increasingly our political debate has devolved into sound bites and slogans as the two major political parties' platforms have ignored the reality of changes overtaking our country.

Tom Friedman and Michael Mandelbaum in their book *That Used to Be Us* describe the Democrats' and Republicans' "war on math," noting that both sides ignore irrefutable financial realities. It is an apt description of the state of our politics today. I have tried in my columns and editorials to use objective, factual analysis, frequently relying on statistical and financial data, to debunk the ideology of the left and right. I have tried not so much to lay out answers but to suggest we are not asking the relevant and often uncomfortable questions.

More often than not, the great public policy issues of our time are complex and the solutions not easy. In a world where the public is hungry for easy answers and the 24-hour media all too eager to provide them, I have tried to swim against the tide. I have asked my readers to lay aside preconceived notions and think harder about the issues facing us.

I have found it interesting that in doing so I have been accused of being a closet member of the other side by about an equal number of Democrats and Republicans—this despite the fact that I frequently proclaim my disdain for both parties and for partisanship generally. But I have also found that notwithstanding the hysterical polarization so prevalent today there is a great center to the American people. I believe it will be the ballast that rights our ship as we continue the great American experiment in self-governance and individual freedom. It has been a great honor and privilege to be that center's voice.

BILL KING
Houston
September 8, 2014

Unapologetically
MODERATE

CHANGING FACE
OF AMERICA
AND THE WORLD

*D*emographic change is sweeping the world, upending societal norms and organizations that have existed since we first began to walk upright. For the first time in our history we are living to unprecedented ages while the birth rate is plummeting. A population array that has always looked like a flattened pyramid will increasingly steepen and probably ultimately inverse. The likelihood that in the not too distant future we will have more old people than young promises to change the world forever.

Also throughout the world, but most acutely in America, the aging of our population is occurring simultaneously with a rapid ethnic diversification. Never before have the various ethnic groups been so interrelated and in such close contact.

A number of American cities, like Houston, are now majority minority communities. By the middle of this century, the country as a whole will be also. How we work out becoming an even more culturally and ethnically diverse society is one of the major challenges for the next several generations. In many ways Houston will be the laboratory for how America will evolve.

My belief in these fundamental demographic changes undergirds many of my columns as I try to anticipate how they will affect particular issues.

A Lesson From Jefferson

I have been reading Jon Meacham's biography of Thomas Jefferson. Meacham says one of the reasons Jefferson was such an outstanding leader was that he knew he stood on a critical fault line of history, when despotic governments that had been the norm since the dawn of civilization were beginning to be replaced by democratic regimes based on individual freedom. And more important, Jefferson was willing to embrace that seismic shift and provide leadership during such a time.

We are living through a similar fault line in history, but unlike Jefferson our leaders are not embracing the inevitable pivot.

This fault line is being brought about by two demographic phenomena that are unique in human history and that will forever change human experience. And they have occurred with such breath-taking rapidity, at least in demographic terms, that we have largely missed them, or at least missed their game-changing implications.

First, in 1970 the life expectancy of a person 65 was 13 years. The life expectancy of a person who is 65 today is 19 years. That is a 50 percent increase in the length of time most of us will be retired. That means the cost of supporting us in our retirement has gone up 50 percent just since 1970. Today an 85-year-old person can expect to live an additional six years. In 1970 the Centers for Disease Control and Prevention did not even calculate a life expectancy for someone 85.

But it is not just the fact that we have longer retirements which must somehow be funded. The cost of caring for retirees has gone up because there has also been an explosion in the level of health care that is now available and that we have come to expect during our later years.

At the same time we have had this incredible increase in life expectancy and healthcare options, the worldwide birth rate has dramatically plummeted. In 1970 the average births per woman, worldwide, was 4.5 children. Today it is 2.3 and continuing to drop. It takes about 2.2 births per woman to maintain a stable population. If the current trend holds, the world's population will top out in about 30 years at around 8 billion to 9 billion people and then start a long-term decline.

Now, the fact that people are living longer, that we can provide healthcare that makes our later life more productive and enjoyable, and that humans are not going to overrun the world are good things. But these changes also have profound societal and public policy implications.

The most basic of these is that the cost of supporting those who are retired is dramatically increasing while fewer and fewer young people will be around to shoulder that burden.

We are already seeing the first signs of this with the financial difficulties various retirement plans face. Whether you are looking at Social Security's long-term sustainability or the massive unfunded pension liabilities many companies and public entities face or how to make your 401k account last the rest of your life, the underlying issue is the same. We simply have no financial models for this conundrum.

And the problem is our leaders want to talk about anything but this elephant in the room. Instead we spend our time debating abortion, amnesty, who we should be able to marry, and who was responsible for the talking points on Benghazi.

The stakes could not be higher. If we continue to fail to deal with this seismic shift, we are not going down in the history books with the glorious approbations history was heaped on Jefferson and the other Founding Fathers. Instead we will be the generation remembered for having failed its children and grandchildren.

May 25, 2013

Population Apocalypse: Part I

W hen I was a sophomore in college, my sociology pro-
fessor had our class read Thomas Malthus' *An Essay on
the Principle of Population*. Malthus argued that human
population increases geometrically while food production only increases arithmetically. Therefore, he concluded that the human race
was destined to eternal misery as its population would always be
bumping up against its ability to produce sustenance.

Malthus wrote his essay around the turn of the 19th century. His
belief that the human race was careening headlong into a population-
induced apocalypse was redefined in modern terms by Paul Ehrlich's
best-selling book, *The Population Bomb*, published in 1968, in which
he predicted worldwide famine in the 1970s and 1980s.

This worldview was reinforced in popular media with movies like
Soylent Green, which depicted a future in which human bodies would
be recycled for food. I remember being so impressed by the danger
they described that I joined a group Ehrlich helped found called Zero
Population Growth.

Malthus' and Ehrlich's dire predictions of famine never came to
pass, primarily due to a burst of agricultural technological advances
in the middle of the 20th century frequently referred to as the Green
Revolution. But until recently, their argument that population grows
geometrically still was thought to be correct. That meant despite the
unanticipated advances in agriculture, the human race still seemed

on a collision course with a world of limited resources, including energy, clean water and arable land.

But a funny thing happened on the way to the population apocalypse: Women across the world suddenly (at least in demographic terms) starting having dramatically fewer babies.

The mathematics of population growth are surprisingly complex, but the basic principle is that there is a direct correlation between population and the average number of children each woman has during her lifetime, which is known as the fertility rate. To maintain a stable population, the average fertility rate must be slightly more than two.

To maintain the population, each woman must have at least two children to replace the mother and the father. But in addition, there must be enough extra children to replace those who die before reaching childbearing age.

When Ehrlich wrote his doomsday prophecy in 1968, the fertility rate was just below five. It had already been slowly declining, but beginning around 1980 it began to plummet and has continued to do so. The World Bank estimates that in 2010, the worldwide fertility rate was down to 2.45. Given the rate of child mortality in developing countries, this is probably not much, if any, above the rate needed to maintain the world's population.

Of course, there are great variations in the fertility rate in different countries. Generally speaking, more developed countries have lower fertility rates while less developed countries have higher rates. For example, the fertility rate in Europe is about 1.5. Japan's is 1.3. The highest rates are found in the desperately poor countries of sub-Saharan Africa and Central Asia. For example, Afghanistan has one of the highest rates in the world at 6.3.

What is perhaps most remarkable is that while some countries still have a high fertility rate, the rates have declined in virtually every country. For example, Afghanistan's rate was nearly 8 just a decade ago.

Most readers will probably be surprised to learn the birth rates in South and Central America have declined dramatically. Almost every country in that region has a fertility rate below the world average. Argentina and Brazil are well below 2. Mexico is only 2.3.

Some countries are facing dramatic population declines. Japan's population, for example, is expected to shrink from around 125 million today to about 90 million by 2050, a loss of almost a third of its population. Japan is now paying subsidies to young couples to have additional babies. Even our population in the U.S. would be headed for decline if it were not for immigration.

The rapidly declining birth rates do not, however, mean that population will not continue to grow for some time. It takes a generation or two for the lower birth rates to work their way through the system, so to speak, as the total number of childbearing-age women today reflects the higher birth rates of 20 years ago. Also, the increase in life expectancy means that the population is not "turning over" as rapidly.

The world's population today is around 7 billion. Most demographers now believe it will top out at around 9 billion between 2040 and 2050.

Thereafter, most forecast a long-term decline. Some believe that the decline in birth rate will continue to accelerate and that population growth will end much sooner.

So it appears that we can all breathe a collective sigh of relief that Malthus' and Ehrlich's apocalyptic prophecies are likely not in our future. But it turns out that stagnant population growth may have its own set of problems. More on that later.

June 20, 2012

Population Apocalypse: Part II

L ast week I discussed some recent demographic trends that suggest the world's population is likely to top out at about 9 billion in the next three to four decades. I noted that many of the doomsday predictions of massive worldwide famines induced by an ever-expanding population have proved to be incorrect and that based on current trends they were unlikely to occur in the future.

I began this discussion because a flattening out of the population is likely to have some consequences that we may not have expected. In fact, I believe that we are already seeing consequences with merely a slowdown in the rate of population growth in programs like Social Security and public pension plans.

But before we begin that discussion, I have tell you something of the response I got to last week's column. There was quite a bit more than usual, most of it challenging the view that the population apocalypse had been avoided.

The reaction fell into two principal groups. First were those who simply refused to believe the population would stabilize and probably begin to decline at some point in the future. One gentleman argued that a 2.0 birth rate on a 9 billion population would produce more population growth than our current 2.4 birth rate on the current world population of 7 billion, apparently confusing the concepts of birth rates and percentage growth. Because it takes two human beings to produce an offspring, every woman must have two children to replace the mother and the father. If that number is less than about 2.2, the population will eventually begin to decline, no matter what the absolute number of people there are in the world. There are various factors that will affect how long it will take for the population growth to slow, but as a pure mathematical matter, it must do so eventually.

The second group insisted that even if the famines have not occurred yet, they and other untold ecological disasters were just around the corner. One reader insisted that Paul Ehrlich was basically correct in his predictions of worldwide famine, just off in his timing.

It is interesting that such doomsday convictions continue to be so widely held when there is so much evidence to the contrary. For several years now, the World Health Organization has maintained we have more obese people in the world than those who are malnourished, a condition that has never existed previously in the human experience. It is also a fact that more humans have access to better health care than ever before. As a result, life expectancies are at all-time highs. Warren Buffet notes that the average American has a higher standard of living in terms of food choices, entertainment options and luxuries than the richest king just 200 years ago. Yet despite the human race's inexorable climb to a higher standard of living by almost any metric, there remains among many an overarching sense of doom.

Obsession over "end times" is nothing new. Most cultures have as part of their belief system some ultimate fate of the human race, with most foreseeing a calamitous end. The beliefs are so widely held that we have a word for such systems: eschatology.

One has to wonder if the explosion of media has exacerbated such fears. The Internet provides a platform to disseminate such theories across a wide audience. I recently saw a website promoting a book that showed how Scripture predicted that the world would end on July 24 of this year. Given how hot it has been in Houston the last few days, I personally am beginning to give some credence to this timetable. The 24-hour cable news cycle adds to the hysteria. Remember how the Gulf would not recover from the BP oil spill for generations or reports on the potential consequences of the Japanese nuclear disaster. Yet neither of these disasters has been in the headlines for months.

Nonetheless, I certainly did not mean to signal the all clear for the human race. Even if we add only 2 billion to the 7 billion here today, that will still entail many formidable challenges. There is a long list of doomsday prophets whose prophecies have been frustrated by unexpected demographic, natural and technological developments. But in the end I am putting my money on the ability of the human race to innovate and adapt.

June 27, 2012

SEVEN BIG ISSUES
WE MUST ADDRESS

*H*ere are seven domestic issues that America has struggled with for the last two decades but has made little progress toward solving:

- *The ever-increasing federal deficit.*
- *Providing retirement income and healthcare to our elderly.*
- *Providing healthcare to everyone else.*
- *Chronic unemployment and under-employment and the decline of the middle class.*
- *Immigration reform.*
- *Mental illness, drugs and addiction.*
- *Climate change and the lack of hurricane preparedness on the Texas Gulf Coast.*

These issues affect virtually every American. They are also in many ways interrelated. In looking at them I have tried to get past ideology, conventional wisdom and partisan talking points. These problems present no easy answers but one. What we are doing is not working.

The Deficit in Perspective

W e have all heard a thousand times: The U.S. is $17 tril-
lion in debt. The number is incomprehensibly large.
Even broken down on a per capita basis, it represents
about $56,000 for every man, woman and child in the country. But
what does it really mean for the U.S. to be $17 trillion in debt?

A good place to begin to try and understand the federal government's finances is a report issued by an obscure federal agency known
as Financial Management Services. The agency actually publishes a
financial report on the federal government each year that contains
the normal information you would expect to see in an annual report.
The most recent report is for the fiscal year ended Sept. 30.

Included in the report is a balance sheet for the federal government. The 2012 balance shows that the federal government has assets
of just below $3 trillion and liabilities of nearly $19 trillion, leaving
a negative net worth of $16 trillion. We know that in the last fiscal
year, the federal government ran a deficit of $600 billion or so, which
presumably will take down the government's net worth by that much
more when the 2013 report is issued. That will make the government
about $16.6 trillion in the red.

However, in addition to these obligations, the surpluses generated by Social Security and Medicare (currently about $3 trillion)
are invested in U.S. treasuries, as are funds held by other agencies.
There are about $5 trillion of these interagency obligations, but under
the accounting rules they are eliminated in a consolidated financial

statement because the federal government, in essence, owes the money to itself. But for the purposes of understanding the debt-ceiling fight that we just went through and seemingly will have to endure *ad nauseam* in the future, the total "federal debt" is the sum of the U.S. Treasury obligations issued to the public and these interagency debts, the total of which is currently about $17 trillion.

The breakdown of what the federal government actually owes will probably be surprising to most. First, the actual amount that the government has borrowed by issuing bonds is only about $12 trillion. The next largest liability is the obligation the federal government has for its pension plans. These plans, unlike most state and local pension plans, are completely unfunded. That is, the federal government has not set aside any money in a separate account to fund the future pension benefits owed to retired federal workers. That obligation, as of 2012, was more than $6 trillion. The balance of the debt, a little more than $1 trillion, includes miscellaneous obligations such as current accounts payable owed by various government agencies to vendors.

It is significant to note that of the new money the federal government "borrows" every year, a significant portion is actually the increase in the unfunded pension obligation. For example, in 2012 the government's liabilities increased by about $1.3 trillion, but nearly $500 billion (38 percent) came in the form of an increase in the pension obligations rather than from selling bonds.

It is also interesting to look at who holds the bonds the government has issued. There seems to be a widespread misconception that China holds most of the debt. But of the $12 trillion of debt held outside the government, China holds only about 10 percent. Japan holds almost as much as China. In all, foreigners hold a little less than half of U.S. securities.

Not included in any of these numbers are the obligations that the federal government has for future Social Security and Medicare benefits in excess of what the taxes for those programs will bring in. Trying to guess at that number is a little tricky. Financial Management Services estimates it at about $35 trillion. Some have estimated it much higher.

The bottom line is that politicians love to reduce issues to sound bites, and normally only those that bolster their political agenda. However, it is simply impossible to reduce the complexity of the federal government's finances to sound bites. It is clear that these future obligations pose a real threat to the prosperity of our future generations. But the extent of that threat and what we should do about it are much murkier.

Because the numbers, when it comes to the federal government's finances, are so incomprehensibly large and because, over time, inflation affects the size of the numbers, economists generally analyze them as a percentage of gross domestic product, or GDP, rather than actual dollar amounts.

GDP, roughly speaking, is the value of all of the goods and services produced by the U.S. economy—our gross income, if you will. Looking at our debt and deficits as a percentage of GDP also allows us to make more accurate comparisons of our conditions to other countries and to previous periods in history.

As of the end of the government's most recent fiscal year, all U.S. securities held by the public are a little more than 70 percent of GDP. If you roll in all of the government's other liabilities, like its unfunded pension obligations, it is more than 100 percent.

Probably the most alarming aspect of this is that the debt as a percent of GDP has doubled since 2006. This has been the result of a combination of the Iraq and Afghanistan wars, a new Medicare prescription benefit, the effects of the recession and the Obama administration's stimulus spending and tax cuts early in his administration.

The only time in the country's history when the debt was higher was immediately after World War II. Prior to 1940, the debt was never more than 40 percent, and the only time it exceeded 20 percent was in times of war.

The federal deficit for last year (i.e., the amount by which all federal expenditures exceeds revenues) was about $600 billion, or about 6 percent of GDP.

When you look at the history of U.S. deficits, there are two very distinct periods. Prior to about 1950, federal deficits were relatively rare, and all except those racked up during the Great Depression were associated with wars.

But after World War II, the federal government began to assume more social welfare responsibility, especially in the area of caring for our elderly. Since that time, the government has run almost continuous deficits. While these tend to ebb and flow with the economy and wars, the trend line definitely is on the up slope.

The average deficit since World War II has been about 2 percent of GDP. The federal deficit for 2009 spiked to 10 percent, the highest non-wartime deficit in the history of the country.

Since then, it has been steadily falling. The Congressional Budget Office projects that by 2015 the deficit will be back down to its post-World War II average of 2 percent. But after that, all bets are off as the baby boomers begin cashing in their Social Security and Medicare benefits. From 2015 forward, the expectation is that there will be an inexorable rise in the deficits and debt.

When it comes to the amount of public debt we owe, the U.S. is pretty much in the middle of the pack when compared with other countries.

Most developed economies have similar debt loads. Japan's debt to GDP is almost three times ours. The United Kingdom, Germany, Canada and France all carry more debt than we do. China and the Scandinavian countries are about half ours. It is a little ironic that these bastions of socialist policies are actually less in debt than we are.

Our 2009 deficit of 10 percent was definitely on the high side compared with other countries, although some like Japan and the U.K. consistently carry larger deficits.

If we succeed in getting ours down to 2 percent by 2015, it will definitely be in the lower range and comparable to our great economic rival/trading partner, China.

When you look at charts of our debt and deficits in nominal terms—that is, the actual dollar amounts—it is hard to not break out in a dead panic.

The lines spike up on the right-hand side of the chart like Mount Everest. And there is no doubt that those trend lines should gravely concern us and spur us to action. But it is also important to remember that appearance of those graphs is skewed by inflation, the Great Recession and because they do not take in account the economy's growth.

When viewed in historical and global context, it is clear that this is not the time to panic and be wildly slashing government spending, as the sequester does.

Rather, we should come up with a plan to deal with the long-term unsustainable trajectory we are on. It would really not be that hard to do if our leaders were really focused on the country's long-term future and not the next election.

October 26 and October 30, 2013

Spending Problem
or Revenue Problem?

T he talking points are repeated *ad nauseam*. Republicans chant over and over that the federal government has a spending problem not a revenue problem, arguing that the federal government's current massive deficits are solely the result of a government spending too much. Democrats incessantly respond that Republicans are cutting critical programs to give tax breaks to millionaires and billionaires, arguing that the deficit is due to a lack of tax revenue. So which is it? Are we spending too much or not taking in enough revenue?

It might be useful first to put the current deficits in some historical perspective. You may be surprised to learn that since World War II the federal budget has been balanced only 12 times. Truman balanced it three times immediately after the war. Eisenhower and Clinton did it three times each as well. Nixon and George W. Bush had balanced budgets in the first year of their presidencies. Truman is the only president since World War II who averaged balancing the budget for his term in office, producing budgets with an average surplus of 1.15 percent of gross domestic product. Prior to Obama, Reagan was the worst, averaging deficits of 4.2 percent.

Overall, Democratic administrations prior to President Obama have averaged deficits of .7 percent of GDP while Republicans averaged deficits of 2.3 percent. While Congress and the economic conditions certainly affect a president's ability to manage the federal budget, it is interesting that the record does not support the generally held notion that Republicans are deficit hawks and Democrats are spendthrifts.

Overall, we have averaged running a deficit of 1.6 percent of GDP each year. Prior to last year, the worst deficit was in 1983 at 6 percent of GDP. The deficits in the first two years of the Obama administration have been 10 percent and 8.9 percent, respectively, and the projected deficit for this fiscal year is 10.9 percent. So the current deficits are truly unprecedented for this country.

The question is: Are these extraordinary deficits the result of out of control spending as the Republicans suggest or are they the result of too little revenue as the Democrats suggest? If we look at revenues and expenditures as a percentage of GDP, the answer would seem to be some of both.

Since 1950 federal government expenses have ranged from 17 percent to 23 percent of GDP. The post-World War II average is 19.5 percent. Before Obama, the high-water mark was in the mid-1980s when expenses were consistently a little over 20 percent, hitting a post-World War II high in 1983 at 23.5 percent. More recently, during the Clinton and George H.W. Bush administrations, federal expenses were generally kept below 20 percent. But in 2009 and 2010 federal expenses rose to 25 percent and 23.8 percent of GDP, respectively. It is projected to rise back to 25 percent this year. Therefore, from a historical perspective, Republicans are correct that our expenses are running about 5 percent more of GDP than "normal."

On the other side of the ledger, since 1950 federal revenues have run 16 percent to 20 percent of GDP. The post-World War II average is 17.8 percent. The highest sustained level of federal receipts was during the latter part of the Clinton administration, when revenues consistently came in close to 20 percent. During the first year of Bush 43's first term, federal receipts barely topped the 20 percent mark.

However, as the Bush tax cuts were implemented, receipts dropped sharply, hitting a low of 16 percent in 2004. The receipts were gradually returning to more typical historic levels when the Great Recession hit. In 2009 and 2010 receipts fell to 14.9 percent for each of those years and are expected to fall farther to 14.4 percent this year. That will tie the post-World War II low recorded in 1950. So from a historical perspective, Democrats are correct that federal receipts are running about 3 percent below "normal." It is a strange phenomenon that the anti-tax Tea Party would be launched and so strongly influence the 2010 election in the midst of a 50-year low in tax receipts.

When you add a 5 percent increase in expenses to a 3 percent decrease in revenues to a historic 2 percent deficit, you end up with about a 10 percent deficit, which is, of course, where we find ourselves today and is clearly unsustainable. This perspective certainly suggests that if we want to balance the budget by returning to historic norms, we have some work to do on both sides of the ledger.

David Walker, former U.S. Comptroller General and now head of the Comeback America Initiative, an advocacy group that focuses on the deficit problem, has been preaching about the impending debt crisis for several years. Walker agrees that we have both a spending and a revenue problem. He has suggested that we need to raise about $1 of revenue for every $3 we cut. It looks to me like 1-to-2 would be a better ratio if your goal is to return to historic norms. But regardless, it is clear that we cannot do everything on just one side of the ledger without abandoning a 60-year formula that has generated one of the most prosperous economies of all times.

May 4, 2011

Debts and Delusions

A few days ago I saw one of the Congressional Tea Party Republicans being interviewed about the federal government. As questions became more adversarial, the congressman's rhetoric amped up. Finally, he shouted to the reporter did he not understand that we were $17 trillion in debt, mostly to the Chinese, and that the federal government was running trillion-dollar annual deficits with no end in sight.

While it is true that the country is $17 trillion in debt, it is certainly not mostly owed to China. In fact, the actual character and structure of the federal debt is complicated, and depending on how you count it, China holds no more than about 10 percent of our debt. But the assertion that the federal government is running trillion-dollar deficits with no end in sight is just flat wrong.

The Congressional Budget Office recently updated its fiscal projections for the federal government. It estimates that the deficit for the fiscal year just ended will be $642 billion. Further, the budget office estimates that the deficit will continue to fall for the next three years, reaching a low of $432 billion in 2016.

After 2016, the deficit begins a slow but inexorable rise as our aging demographics continually push up the costs of Social Security and Medicare. However, even then the Congressional Budget Office projections do not show the deficit reaching a trillion dollars again during its forecast period, which goes through 2023.

Even more important than the gross numbers is the deficit as a share of the gross domestic product—roughly speaking, the value of all goods and services produced by the U.S. economy.

Since World War II, we have averaged running a deficit of about 2 percent of the GDP, although the trend line has been ramping up gradually. The average since 1980 has been about 2.6 percent.

In 2012, the last year for which the books are closed, the deficit was slightly more than a trillion dollars, which was 6.8 percent of GDP, or a little less than three times the recent average. But for 2013, if the deficit comes in at $642 billion as the budget office expects, the percentage will drop to just under 4 percent. And over the next three years, the deficit will drop to a little over 2 percent of GDP. This level would be consistent with recent historical averages and less than half the deficit the federal government carried during the Reagan administration.

There are a couple of ironies here. First, if the budget office projections are accurate, the average deficit during the Obama administration will be only about half a percent higher than during the Reagan administration. This fact should probably remind us that any president has much less control over the amount of the deficit than we are prone to believe. Second, the truth is that notwithstanding the dysfunction in Washington the president and Congress have actually stumbled into a pretty good fix of our fiscal challenges—at least in the short-term.

The Democrats' insistence on additional revenues and the Republicans' insistence on spending cuts have returned the level of revenues and expenses pretty close to historical averages. But instead of taking a bow for getting the deficit dramatically reduced, both sides continue to amp up the rhetoric, leaving impression that the government is on the verge of collapse.

But there is nothing in the budget office projections that should be interpreted as an "all clear" signal. The problem we are facing is not the deficits over the next few years. The problem is the long-term sustainability of our entitlement programs. The challenge there primarily is the result of fundamental demographic changes: Americans are living longer and having fewer babies. Those two trends mean that the burden of taking care of our elders is going to be greater on future generations. Because we have by and large shifted the burden of caring for seniors to the federal government, that growing commitment is showing up as a long-term fiscal problem.

And that is the conversation we need to be having: How do we humanely care for our seniors over the next few decades without destroying the lifestyles and dreams of our children and our grandchildren? All the histrionics and political posturing we are currently enduring are a distraction from addressing this fundamental, long-term challenge.

October 9, 2013

Is Social Security a Ponzi Scheme?

Texas Gov. Rick Perry set off a political firestorm worse than those currently burning in Central Texas when he recently referred to Social Security as a "Ponzi scheme" and a "monstrous lie." The political stakes could not be higher. Americans have very strong feelings—but not totally consistent views—on Social Security.

Polls consistently show very high levels of support for the program across all age groups. But in a recent CNN poll, 81 percent of respondents agreed that Social Security would face financial difficulties if it was not changed. Is Perry's rhetoric or the public's concerns about Social Security justified?

Social Security generally refers to two programs. The Old Age and Survivors Insurance (OASI) pays pension benefits to older Americans. The Disability Insurance (DI) pays benefits to disabled Americans. At the end of 2010 about 44 million Americans were receiving benefits from OASI and about 10 million from DI. Total expenditures for the programs including benefits and administrative costs for 2010 were $713 billion, or about 20 percent of all federal government expenditures.

Social Security benefits are mainly financed by a payroll tax. When Social Security was first implemented in 1937, the payroll tax rate was 2 percent and applied to only the first $3,000 of income annually. It has risen steadily since that time to the current rate of 12.4 percent of a person's wages or salary up to a maximum of $106,800. As a bookkeeping matter, we say that half of the tax (6.2 percent) is paid by the employer and the other half by the employee. Economists, however, will tell you that the employee really pays 100 percent of the cost because without the tax, wages would rise by that amount.

The income that Social Security has received in excess of its expenses has been placed into separate trust funds for the payment of pensions and disability benefits. At the end of 2010, there was about $2.4 trillion in the OASI trust fund and $179 billion in the DI trust fund. In addition to the income that Social Security receives from the payroll tax, it also earns interest on the investment of these trust funds. In 2010, Social Security earned $117 billion in interest payments.

Part of the controversy surrounding Social Security is how these trust funds are invested. In regular pension plans the income would be invested in a variety of stocks and bonds to both diversify the risk and maximize the return. However, all of Social Security's income is invested in U.S. securities. So the federal government is collecting the payroll tax and then loaning itself the excess.

You may have heard critics of Social Security allege that there is no money in the Social Security and that Congress has already spent all of the money paid into the system. Since the federal government has used the proceeds to finance its ongoing expenditures, the criticism is in some sense true. But on the other hand, U.S. securities are recognized by the market as one of the safest investments in the world.

In a classic Ponzi scheme, the promoter sells some kind of investment units to the victims. Instead of investing the money as promised, the promoter uses a portion of the money to pay phony returns to the investors and pockets the rest. To pay the next round of returns the promoter must bring in additional investors. As the scheme grows, mathematics dictates that the number of investors needed to pay the previous investors will grow geometrically; hence the scheme is also frequently referred to as a pyramid scheme.

The key element to a Ponzi scheme is that the promoter is lying to the investors about how their money is being used. The result of a Ponzi scheme is that it will eventually fail because eventually the number of new investors needed to continue to fund the scheme will become unsustainable. To fairly call Social Security a Ponzi scheme, one would have to conclude that the federal government is not using the contributions as it has promised and that the system is growing geometrically and is therefore unsustainable over time.

There is no question that Social Security's income is first used to pay benefits and that the balance is invested in U.S. securities. So unless one is prepared to argue that U.S. securities are not a legitimate investment, it is hard to argue that the federal government is not using the funds as represented to the participants in Social Security. And in that sense, Social Security is clearly not a classic Ponzi scheme.

However, if the comparison of Social Security to a Ponzi scheme is made for the purpose of arguing it is unsustainable over time, that may be more accurate.

In 2010 Social Security received $661 billion from payroll taxes and income taxes on benefits. It paid out $702 billion in benefits and about another $11 billion in administrative and other miscellaneous expenses. But as I noted above, it also received $117 million in interest payments from the federal government on the U.S. securities in the trust fund, leaving a small surplus for the year of $69 billion.

This is fairly typical of the plan's performance since the late 1950s. For the first 20 years after Social Security was adopted in 1937, the payroll tax receipts substantially exceeded the benefits paid. In 1959 the benefits paid exceeded the fund's income for the first time. Since the late 1950s the ratio of the payroll taxes collected and the benefits paid have ranged from approximately 85 percent to 105 percent. Over the 70 years of Social Security's existence it has received income of approximately $14 trillion and paid out $11.5 trillion in benefits, leaving the current balance in the trust fund of approximately

$2.5 trillion.

Because Social Security has been paying nearly all of the income in benefits for most of its existence, it never has been, in the traditional sense, a retirement savings system. In a true retirement saving account, the contributions would be segregated and invested in a diversified portfolio. The combination of periodic contributions and earnings on those contributions then becomes a corpus available to support the participants during their retirement.

Social Security in contrast has from its inception been a vehicle to transfer income between generations. It is, at its essence, the institutionalization at the national level of what humans have done for millennia at the family or tribal level. Younger members of society take care of those who can no longer take care of themselves.

However, the sustainability of this model was based on the fact that, until the last few decades, most humans did not survive for very long after their "retirement." When Social Security was adopted in 1937, the average life expectancy at 65 was about 12 years. Today it is closer to 20 years. That increase in life expectancy not only about doubles the cost of the benefits paid to each recipient but also increases the number of recipients.

In the early days of Social Security, the ratio of workers paying into the system compared to the number of beneficiaries was very high because of the procedures used to phase in the benefits initially. By 1960 the ratio of workers to beneficiaries had stabilized at about 5:1. However, it has steadily worsened since then and in 2010 fell to just below 3:1.

That may not seem like much of change, but combined with the cost of the benefits almost doubling from longer life expectancies, it means that for the average worker the burden of the system has tripled since 1960. And that is not even considering the various increases to benefits that Congress has granted over time. To further complicate the situation, these demographic trends get worse over the next several decades since we expect that life expectancies will continue to lengthen and birth rates to decline.

The basic facts regarding how the system works, including its long-term funding challenges, are plainly disclosed by Social Security's annual report. See http://www.ssa.gov/oact/trsum/index.html. If people are misinformed about the status of Social Security, it is because they have not taken the time to inform themselves, not because someone has lied to them.

Also, the funds are used precisely as the law provides. They are first used to pay benefits, with the excess being invested in U.S. securities. There are those who contend that the government's investing the excess proceeds in its own notes is a fraud, but that argument has no merit. If any pension manager invested 100 percent of a pension's assets in U.S. securities, one might quarrel with his investment strategy, but it certainly would not constitute fraud.

Social Security's funding problems are purely a result of the fact that our demographics have changed and we have not sufficiently modified the program to reflect those changes because it is politically painful to do so.

September 14 and September 21, 2011

State of the System Today

E ach year, Social Security issues an annual report that includes an actuary study examining the long-term prospects for the program. The current report projects the performance of the program through 2085, approximately the average life expectancy at birth of everyone living today.

To predict how Social Security will work in the future, the actuaries must make assumptions about birth rates, life expectancies, unemployment, inflation, interest rates, annual immigration and dozens of other factors. Predicting any of these for even a few years is a challenge. Attempting to predict such outcomes over the next 75 years borders on hubris.

To give some nod to the obvious uncertainty of making such long-term projections, Social Security's actuaries make assumptions over a range and have developed a best, worst and middle case for Social Security's future based the system's current taxes. The numbers I discuss below are the actuaries' middle case and assume that we make no changes to the benefits that are currently being paid or the taxes that support the system.

For 53 of Social Security's 70 years, the payroll taxes paid into the system have exceeded benefits paid out. Unfortunately, those days are gone. In 2010 Social Security collected about $49 billion less in taxes than its expenses and what it paid out in benefits. It is clear that benefits will continue to outstrip payroll taxes indefinitely into the future.

Currently, the gap between benefits and payroll taxes is more than made up by the interest payments Social Security receives from the U.S. bonds it holds as a result of the previous surpluses. However, the actuaries project that by 2022 the benefits will exceed both the payroll taxes and the interest payments and that the program will have to begin to liquidate its holdings of U.S. bonds.

There are those who maintain that Social Security's holdings of U.S. bonds are worthless and that the government will not, or will not be able to, pay off the bonds as they become due. This is a view to which I most decidedly do not subscribe. For the purposes of our analysis today, I will assume that federal government will be able to pay off the bonds that Social Security holds as they become due.

In that event, the actuaries project that Social Security will exhaust its bond holdings in 2036. By that time, the payroll taxes that the program will be collecting will be equal to about 90 percent of the current benefits. At that point, the federal government will either have to start making transfers from the general fund to support the program (as it currently does with Medicare) or the benefits will have to be reduced to about 90 percent of the current level. Beyond 2036, the ratio by which the benefits outstrip the payroll taxes gradually worsens. From 2036 through 2085, the actuaries project that Social Security will be able to pay only about 75 percent of the current benefits.

The projected funding gap is driven entirely by worsening demographics. As birth rates continue to decline and life expectancies lengthen, the ratio of workers to retirees continues to decline. The current projection is that by 2085 there will be only about two workers for each retiree.

While the picture of Social Security's future painted by the actuaries is not particularly cheery, it is hardly the unfolding catastrophe one would expect from the current political angst and rhetoric over the subject. Social Security can be sustained with some relatively minor, incremental changes that can be implemented over a fairly long time horizon, especially if we commit to those changes now.

There is, however, one caveat. There are significant risks in defining a benefit today to be paid in the future. The actuaries' projections are not much more than educated guesses, and relatively small changes in their assumptions can dramatically affect the outcomes.

There are also wild cards that could play havoc on the system. For example, suppose that tomorrow someone comes up with a cure for cancer. It would be great day for humanity but a disaster for Social Security. Such a breakthrough would radically alter the life expectancy assumptions used by the actuaries, and we would exhaust the program's savings sooner and be able to pay out only a much smaller percentage of the current benefits thereafter.

As a result, we should all be mindful that Social Security never has been and never will be a system of true retirement saving accounts. The money we paid into the system did not go into an account somewhere to be held until we needed it. It went to our parents and grandparents to support them in their retirement. In doing so, we have been relieved of some of the full burden of providing for our predecessor generations. Hopefully our children and grandchildren will do the same for us. But we have to be realistic about the amount of the burden we place on their shoulders.

September 28, 2011

Trusting the Trust Funds

S ince 1937 when Social Security was adopted, Congress has generally set the payroll tax rate slightly higher than what has been needed to pay Social Security benefits. As result, Social Security has accumulated a surplus of about $2.6 trillion, which it has invested in U.S. bonds.

In March 2011 Sen. Tom Coburn (R-OK) in a speech on the Senate floor alleged that "Congresses under both Republican and Democrat control, both Republican and Democrat presidents, have stolen money from Social Security and spent it. The money's gone. It's been used for another purpose."

Sen. Coburn's message resonated with the Internet conspiracy crowd and has been often repeated. While the senator's description of how Social Security cash flows is roughly correct, his analysis that the money has been "stolen" is dead wrong and sends us off in the wrong direction in trying to fix the system.

Sen. Coburn implies that if Social Security's surplus funds had just been invested in something other than U.S. bonds, the program would be OK today. Nothing could be further from the truth, and such implications obfuscate the underlying demographic issues that are the real challenge for Social Security's long-term viability.

Sen. Coburn is wrong for two reasons.

First, U.S. bonds held by Social Security are not worthless and not likely to become worthless any time in the near future. The assertion that Social Security bonds are worthless is based in part on the fact that its U.S. bonds are a special, non-negotiable issue. That is, Social Security is prohibited from selling the bonds. But since Social Security has no intention or need to sell the bonds, that restriction is irrelevant.

The U.S. bonds held by Social Security have maturities that range from one to 15 years. The average interest rate is set by formula adopted by Congress. The average weighted return on the portfolio in 2010 was 4.6 percent. If the restriction on selling the bonds were lifted, Social Security could sell many of them at a substantial profit, since they were issued at an earlier time when interest rates were higher than the current market rates.

Sen. Coburn and the other "they-stole-the-Social-Security-money" buffs never address what investment other than U.S. bonds they would have preferred. Enron stock perhaps? After the federal government's brilliant Solyndra investment, do we really want the feds picking stocks?

But the real issue is whether the federal government will be able to make its interest payments and retire the principal of the bonds as they become due over the next 15 years. Certainly the markets believe it will be able to do so. Currently, 30-year U.S. bonds are being snapped up at historically low interest rates. Most auctions of U.S. securities result in two to three times as many bids as bonds available for sale. So while anything is possible, the best financial minds in the world are betting trillions of dollars that the U.S. government will not default on its debt for the next 30 years.

But here is the main thing: Even if the U.S. bonds held by Social Security were really worthless and we wrote them off tomorrow, it would have relatively little impact on the program. If Social Security could not count on the interest income or principal repayment from these bonds, and if Congress was not willing to increase the payroll tax, current benefits would have to be reduced by about 5 percent.

Through 2036, benefits would have to be further gradually reduced to about 90 percent of their current level. Beyond 2036, the actuarial projection would not change since it is assumed that the bond portfolio would be exhausted by that point in any event.

The reason the trust fund has such a relatively small impact on Social Security long-term results is because Social Security is not, and was not from its inception, a retirement savings accounts where the payroll taxes paid into the system were invested to create a fund for each worker's retirement. Rather, Social Security is a social compact that younger generations will devote some portion of their income to provide an income for retired Americans. The money you have paid into the system did not go to create an account for you; it went to provide benefits for your parents and your grandparents.

October 12, 2011

What Needs to Be Done?

In a perfect world, each individual would save enough during his or her career to be self-sufficient in retirement. In the real world, few people are able to do so or ever have. Instead our species has settled on a social contract that younger generations will provide for their elders in their retirement. For millennia, this social contract was carried out at the family or tribal level.

In 1937 America institutionalized this arrangement at the national level with the adoption of Social Security. Social Security is not a retirement savings accounts program nor is it insurance. It is simply a device to transfer income from the working generations to the retired generations. Comparisons of Social Security to retirement savings accounts are misguided.

It is a system that has worked well over the last 70 years. It has provided an income base for retired Americans at a level that has been tolerable for the working generations and has done so with nominal administrative expenses.

However, because of falling birth rates and long life expectancies, the current benefits provided by Social Security are becoming unsustainable. When Social Security was working best, there were 4.5 workers for every retiree. In 2010 that ratio fell for the first time to just below 3:1, and the actuaries project that it will continue to decline for the balance of this century.

There are really only two ways to address this problem. We can either raise the payroll taxes that finance Social Security benefits, or we can reduce benefits. We can dance around this issue all we want, but ultimately one of these two courses (or some combination of the two) will be required to save the system.

There have been scores of proposals for how taxes should be increased or benefits reduced. The Office of the Chief Actuary for Social Security has run models on many of these proposals. The results can be found at http://www.ssa.gov/oact/solvency/provisions/index.html.

The idea of raising the current payroll taxes rate of 12.4 percent would seem problematic. We already heavily tax employment, which encourages the deployment of technology to replace workers. If the tax is increased, there would likely be further pressure on employment, which is something the economy can hardly afford and might actually make the Social Security situation worse.

A better case can be made for increasing the maximum amount on which Social Security taxes is paid. That maximum is currently $106,800. The actuarial projections predict that removing this maximum completely would solve Social Security's long-term sustainability. Of course, this would represent a massive tax increase for those earning over the maximum, a group already shouldering most of the income tax burden.

The other factor that makes a large difference is raising the eligibility age for benefits. Originally a person could retire with full benefits at 65. (There is an option to retire at 62 with reduced benefits.) For individuals born after 1942, the retirement age was raised to 66. For those who are currently younger than 57, the retirement age is scheduled to gradually increase to 67. However, this is clearly not enough.

When Social Security was originally adopted, the average life expectancy at 65 was about 12 years. Therefore, the average worker would collect benefits for about 25 percent of the years he or she paid into the system. However, today the average life expectancy at 65 is nearly 20 years, which means that a worker would be on retirement for 42 percent of their working career. By 2085 it is projected to be 24 years, raising the ratio to nearly 47 percent.

We need to gradually begin increasing the retirement age with a goal of getting back closer to ratio of 25 percent to 30 percent. The retirement age would have to be raised to around 70 to accomplish this goal. The actuaries project that if the retirement age was gradually raised to 70 between now and 2085, there would be significant improvement in Social Security's long-term sustainability, but the trust fund would still be exhausted by about 2045. Obviously a more accelerated schedule increasing the retirement age would have a greater effect.

There are host of other potentials fixes such as lowering the monthly benefits, eliminating or limiting cost of living increases, increasing the taxation of benefits, and alternative investments of the trust funds to earn a higher rate of return. Fixing our immigration policy would also have a beneficial effect. But two changes that seem to be the best candidates for reforming the system are some combination of increasing the income subject to the payroll tax and increasing the retirement age.

The good news about Social Security is that it is not in an immediate crisis. Unlike Medicare, it does not contribute to the current federal deficit. We have some time to get this fixed, and we have the luxury of making relatively small, incremental changes. There is no need for radical changes to the system.

But Social Security must be reformed to be sustainable over the long run. And as with most problems, the sooner we get started the easier and less painful it will be to make the necessary changes.

October 19, 2011

Social Security as Entitlement

A retired reader emailed not long ago complaining that I referred to Social Security as an entitlement. He argued that he had paid into the system for his entire career and had, thus, earned the Social Security benefits he was receiving. Of course, the implication of his complaint is that an entitlement is something that is not earned. Since the word is derived from feudal titles that were "given" by the king, perhaps the implication is fair.

Whether individuals have been given or have earned their Social Security benefits raises the question of how their contributions over the span of their working life compare to the benefits they receive during their retirement. As it turns out, the answer varies greatly based on the individual's circumstances.

The Social Security Administration periodically calculates the rate of return of Social Security benefits on a number of hypothetical scenarios, with the rates ranging from a high of about 9 percent to a low of just over 1 percent. That is, for their range of scenarios we all get back all of the money we put into Social Security and something between 1 percent and 9 percent interest on the contributions we have made.

Outcomes vary based on income level, marital status and longevity. Low-income workers where only one person works come out the best. Couples with high incomes where both spouses work come out the worst.

It is important to keep in mind that these scenarios are based on averaging various variables. The most important variable is how long people live after they begin receiving benefits. The longer a person lives, the more benefits he or she will receive and the higher the rate of return on their contributions. While the actual break-even point varies dramatically, generally speaking you need to make it to about 75 to get back the money you paid into the system.

Currently only about 25 percent of Americans die before the age of 75. That means about 75 percent of Social Security participants will get back more out of the system than they put in, before considering the time value of money.

The 1 percent to 9 percent rates of return assume the person will live to a normal life expectancy, which is in the low 80s today. If you make it past your early 80s, the rate of return goes up substantially.

So that brings me back to my reader's complaint about referring to Social Security as an entitlement. And to the extent that word suggests the benefits are given to someone as opposed to being earned, it is an incorrect description for most retirees, because even at a 9 percent return, the benefits can hardly be considered to have been "given."

I suspect the reader also objected to Social Security benefits being lumped in with other welfare benefits that are clearly not earned. Increasingly I have seen the term "transfer payments" used instead of entitlements. It is probably a more accurate descriptor, although my reader may not find it much less objectionable.

The term transfer payment is, nonetheless, technically correct because Social Security is not a retirement saving account like traditional pension plans or 401k accounts. In those plans, the participants or their employers contribute each year to the plans and those contributions are set aside and invested to create a fund that will be available in the future to provide a retirement income.

In the case of Social Security, however, that plan began paying benefits essentially immediately. The payroll taxes paid in those early days did not go to create an investments account for the workers. Instead they went to pay benefits to workers' parents and grandparents, who had not paid into the system. Since then every generation has been paying for the previous generation.

Thus, Social Security is, and always has been, a transfer of income between generations. The money you and I paid into Social Security did not go to create an account for us somewhere. It went to support our parents and our grandparents.

Certainly to the extent my reader objects to putting Social Security in the same category as welfare payments, he has a valid point. The fact that payments into the system did not actually create a savings account somewhere is irrelevant. Participants earned the right to expect the same support from the next generation they provided to the previous one, even if some modifications in benefits have to be made to accommodate our changing demographics.

November 13, 2013

Don't Look for Villains

It is basic human nature when we learn of a serious problem to want to know whom to blame. This is especially the case when we are blindsided by the problem. Increasingly I am seeing this occur with taxpayers as they are coming to realize how enormously in debt they have become to public employees because of massive unfunded pension promises.

I saw the same thing in the savings and loan crisis in the 1980s. As that once venerable industry collapsed, the generally accepted narrative was that "S&L crooks" had ransacked the institutions. Three decades later, virtually every expert who has studied the problem has concluded that fraud and abuse made up a tiny fraction of the industry's losses and that the real cause of the collapse was the unintended, but nonetheless disastrous, consequences of well-intended government policies and changed markets.

So it is with the public pension mess we now find ourselves.

Have spineless politicians contributed to the problem by making promises to public employees but failing to ask the taxpayers to fund those promises? Absolutely. Have public employee groups in some cases used their political clout to overreach and get unrealistic benefits? Absolutely. Have cases of abuse, and perhaps even fraud, occurred in the upper echelon of some plans? Absolutely. Are any of these the reason we face a looming crisis with respect to these plans today? Absolutely not. In some cases such factors may be contributing to the severity of the problem, but even if every plan had been pristinely run, we would still be facing a crisis.

The current problems have primarily arisen from changes in demographics and the financial markets that were beyond the control of any of the participants and for which no one is fairly to blame.

At the core of the pension problem is the same issue that is threatening the long-term viability of Social Security—we are living a lot longer. Most public pensions originated in the first half of the 20th century when life expectancies were significantly lower. As late as 1970, the average life expectancy at 50, an age at which many public sector employees have been able to retire, was an additional 23 years. By 2008 a 50-year-old could expect to live for an additional 31 years. This rise in life expectancy alone increased the cost of a defined pension benefit by about a third.

Another factor that has weighed heavily on the financial viability of these plans is the slow-down in the growth of public sector jobs. Defined benefit plans work best when there is an ever-growing base of younger employees to contribute to the plan. From 1960 to 2000 public sector employment in the United States more than doubled. But since 2000 it has hit a brick wall. Between 2000 and 2011 public sector employment averaged growing by less than one-half percent and has actually been falling since 2008.

This again is being driven by some fundamental demographics. For example, the U.S. crime rate has been steadily falling for the last two decades. As a result constant demands from the public for more "boots on the ground" have subsided and the growth in police forces with them. The Justice Department conducts a survey of state and local law enforcement agencies every four years. It found that from 1996 to 2000, the number of officers at these agencies grew by 17 percent percent. By the 2004 survey the rate had dropped to 10 percent and even farther in 2008 to 7 percent. Based on looking at some individual departments' numbers, I would not be surprised to see the

2012 survey come in flat.

The same is true for the fire services. The total number of fires reported in the United States has been steadily declining in the last decade as fire prevention technology has improved. Just since 2003 residential fires have dropped by 7 percent. As a result, the total number of firefighters in the country has averaged growing by only about one-half of 1 percent since 1986 and declined last year for the first time in many decades.

In addition to the demographic changes, there have been fundamental shifts in capital markets. For most of their history, defined benefit pensions could invest their assets very conservatively and still produce enough income to pay the promised benefits. From 1970 to 2000, short-term treasury securities yielded over 6 percent, which was about what the actuaries said these plans needed to stay viable. However, since 2000 the same short-term treasuries have yielded less than 2 percent.

The bottom line is this. We have public pension plans that were adopted with the best of intentions. But circumstances have changed. In the new reality in which we find ourselves today, their structure is no longer viable. We can react to this in one of three ways. We can stick our heads in the sand and pretend there is no problem. We can start conducting witch-hunts to find someone to blame. Or we can sit down like adults and find a new way forward that will be fair, realistic and generationally responsible. It will be interesting to see which path we choose.

February 22, 2012

Pensions and Investment Returns

I n a defined benefit pension plan, the employer promises to pay its employees a pension on their retirement. While plans vary greatly, generally pensions are based on some percentage of the employees' compensation near the end of their employment and are paid for life.

To make sure the employer will have the money make the pension payments in the future, money is set aside each year into a trust from which the future payments will be made. Normally both the employer and the employees contribute to the money being set aside annually. While the three city of Houston plans vary somewhat, last year on average the city put up $3 for every $1 contributed by the employees. The actuaries project that by 2022 the city will be contributing about $6 for every $1 contributed by the employees.

This money is then invested, and investment earnings are added to the account. Typically the money will be held for 20 to 30 years before the benefit begins to be paid, which means the investment earnings are a critical component of making the plans work. Generally the investment earnings will make up about 60 percent of the money in the account. So the rate that the trust earns very much affects whether there will be enough money to make the pension payments due to the employees.

To make some guess at how much money should be set aside each year, the actuaries must make an assumption about what the plans will earn on their investments over the next 20-30 years. Of course, no one knows, so the trustees of the plans set an investment goal that the actuaries use.

Here's where it gets a little tricky. The higher the assumed rate, the more money the actuaries will assume the plans will have in the future and the less the city will have to put in. The lower the assumed rate, the more money the city has to contribute.

That means it is actually in the employees' best interests to use as low an assumed rate as possible to make sure the city is putting in enough money each year.

A few decades ago, the argument between state and local governments and their employees generally involved government complaints that the assumed rate was too low. So you may find it curious that the trustees for all three of Houston's pension plans have set the assumed rate at 8.5 percent, the highest used by any pension plan in the United States. A study conducted in 2012 by the National Association of State Retirement Administrators found less than 3 percent of plans surveyed used an 8.5 percent assumption. The state of Illinois, another well-known bastion of financial stability, also uses an 8.5 percent rate.

You might be wondering at this point why in the world would the trustees be using the highest rate in the country. The answer is that using a high rate minimizes the cost of the plans and masks how deeply the city is in debt to the plans. If a lower rate were used, it would be even more apparent that the city cannot afford these plans.

Even at the 8.5 percent rate, the city has not come up with enough money to fully fund the pensions for the last 15 years. Last year alone the actuaries calculated the city needed to contribute about $310 million, but the city put in only $240 million, kicking the can down the road on about $70 million. If, say, a 7.5 percent assumed rate had been used, the city would have been short by nearly another $100 million. And instead of being $2.6 billion in debt to the plans, the city would owe $3.7 billion.

Here is the important thing for Houston taxpayers to understand. The assumed rate makes no difference in the actual liability for future pension payments. Whether the plans earn 1 percent or 10 percent, the employees are going to get the same pension regardless of the investment performance of the plans. It is an inherent characteristic of a defined benefit plan that the future investment risk to borne by the employer and not the employees, precisely the opposite of defined contribution plans. If the plans miss the target, you, the Houston taxpayers, will pick up the difference.

That is why the leaders of these plans are so manic to convince the public and their members that the assumed rate is achievable. They know that if it becomes apparent that the plans will earn something less than 8.5 percent, the gargantuan costs of these plans become even more astronomical, increasing the risk of taxpayer backlash and the loss of confidence of the employee participants.

Here is some idea of the magnitude of an 8.5 percent rate of return: Assuming all of the assets were invested in Dow Jones stocks that pay a 2 percent dividend, the Dow Jones index, currently around 15,000, would have to rise to more than 26,000 in the next 10 years to meet this goal. By 2050, it would have to reach 180,000.

And the consequences of missing the investment goal are severe. If that assumption is off by just 1 percent and the plans earn only 7.5 percent, the current annual cost would go up by around $100 million and the current debt would balloon to almost $4 billion.

It is inherently a fool's errand to attempt to estimate future rates of return, especially over the decades that the benefits under these plans will be paid. But if you are going to run a defined benefit pension plan, it is an errand on which you must embark. So what do other pension plans assume will be a reasonable rate of return?

The 2012 survey by the pension industry group found that the average assumption was 7.8 percent. Most other investment experts doubt that pension plans will be able to achieve rates of 8 percent or more. Warren Buffet, arguably the most successful investor of all time, has said that 6 percent was a reasonable assumption and that a rate of 8 percent was "crazy."

Administrators of the city's three pension plans argue that their rate is reasonable because, historically, they earned more than the projected 8.5 percent. Of course, past performance is no guarantee of future returns, but even if it were, trying to analyze what the plans have earned in the past is more difficult than one might expect.

This is true because the plans have been experiencing very high volatility since the early 1980s and especially in the past decade. From the information that is publicly available, the plans have earned as much as 44 percent in one year and lost as much as 20 percent in others.

The plans' administrators are fond of using averages over time to justify their assumptions. The problem with averages is that they can be highly manipulated based on the time period chosen. For example, if you look at the firefighters fund over the past three years, the plan earned 13.3 percent, easily outperforming the goal. But that is the average for 2010-12, when the market was recovering. If you stretch the average back to include 2008 and 2009, the average drops to 4.8 percent.

It is true that if we look back over longer time horizons, the plans have generally exceeded the 8.5 percent goal. For just about any time period over 10 years, all of the plans average in the 9 percent to 10 percent range. However, if you draw a trend line through the plans' averages over the past several decades, there is noticeable decline. So, is it possible rates are going to return to the previous levels and the plans will make their 8.5 percent goal? Certainly, it is possible. But there is a very substantial risk that they will miss the goals.

Plan administrators, notwithstanding their bluster to the contrary, clearly are aware of this. We know that because they are not willing to assume the investment risk. If the administrators are as confident as they claim, they should jump at the chance to make a profit if they exceed the 8.5 percent by transferring the investment risk from the taxpayer to themselves.

I would not hold my breath.

August 21 and August 24, 2013

Advice to Public Employees

S everal years ago I worked with a number of other Houstonians to form the Fire Fighters Foundation of Houston. Since its organization, the foundation has raised more than $1 million to fund the purchase of specialized equipment and training facilities for the Houston Fire Department.

Because of my support for the fire department through the foundation, many firefighters were dismayed when I began to call attention to the problems with the city of Houston pension plans. I had breakfast last year with a group of fire fighters to try and explain what they saw as a contradiction between my support for their foundation and my concerns about the city's pension plans.

What I shared with them that morning was this simple fact: Financially unsustainable pensions are a bad deal for public employees. This is true because eventually, as it becomes more apparent to the public that the pensions are unsustainable, it will lead to a fight between taxpayers and public employees. And the public employees are going to lose that fight every time.

There was a great deal of skepticism regarding my views that morning, but I believe the election results in Wisconsin and California last week have shown I was correct.

In Wisconsin, of course, Scott Walker handily held off a recall effort organized by public employee unions angry about his moves to limit their powers. In San Jose and San Diego, the issue was put even more sharply in focus. In both cities voters were asked to approve substantial cuts in public employee pensions. In both cases, the ballot initiatives were approved by more than a 2-to-1 margin.

National polling shows similar attitudes across the country. One poll showed that 64 percent of Americans were opposed altogether to unions for public employees. Surprisingly, in that poll over 42 percent of self-identified Democrats agreed with the majority.

We had a harbinger of this trend in Houston in 2004. The 2003 Texas Legislature approved a constitutional amendment prohibiting cities from changing pension benefits for current employees. However, the amendment contained a provision that allowed cities to opt out of the effect of the amendment if voters approved. Then newly elected Mayor Bill White called just such an election in May 2004. Houston voters approved opting out of the amendment guaranteeing pension benefits with over 70 percent of the vote.

Many factors are working against public employees on this issue. First, the vast majority of private sector employees no longer have defined benefit plans. According to the Department of Labor, as of 2009 there were only 18 million Americans who were active participants in a defined benefit plan in the private sector, and that number is dropping rapidly.

Second, state and local governments have really felt the fiscal pinch in the last downturn. As a result, they have frequently been forced to choose between funding their pensions and shortchanging other services. Increasingly the public is beginning to connect the dots between ballooning pension costs and shorter library hours, fewer police on the street and a variety of other cutbacks.

Finally, there was a time when higher public sector pensions could be justified because public sector wages were so much lower than in the private sector. But over the last 20 years, private sector wages have stagnated while public sector compensation has been pushed steadily higher, mostly due to automatic cost of living increases. The most recent data from the Bureau of Labor Statistics shows that the total cost (including wages and benefits) of the average private sector employee at about $29 per hour, which is well below the average for state and local employees at $41 per hour.

What is now a growing public concern over the public pension problems will ultimately turn to outrage at the ballot box. The actuarial reports for the city of Houston's pension plans show that by 2020 it will take nearly 50 percent of the city's property tax receipts just fund the required pension plan contributions. One can only imagine the kinds of service cuts and tax increases it will require to sustain the plans at that point.

As I shared with my friends in the fire department at breakfast last year, if I was in a leadership position in a public employee union, I would try to get out ahead of this issue and propose some reasonable reforms. Simply sticking one's head in the sand and hoping the Dow is going to 20,000 to save these plans is a recipe for disaster. And it will be a disaster for both taxpayers and public employees. Only, as last week's elections prove, the taxpayers will have the last word.

June 13, 2012

Solving the Mess

Notwithstanding the mind-numbing complexity of the city of Houston employee pension morass, the path out of it is fairly clear and can be summed up by two well-worn adages:

1. When you are in a hole, stop digging.
2. Keep your word.

In just over a decade, we have gone from pension plans that were overfunded to ones that will have a shortfall of more than $5 billion by 2020. When you have dug yourself that deep of a hole, the most important thing is to stop digging.

The fairest way to do that is to stop offering new city employees defined benefit pension plans. This does not solve the problem. But it does, at least, keep it from getting worse.

And there is no good reason not to stop offering defined benefit plans. The private sector began making the switch to defined contribution plans 20 years ago. Today, a defined benefit plan is almost unheard-of in the private sector.

There are those who argue that you will not be able to recruit qualified employees without a defined benefit plan. There is scant evidence to support that view. For example, senior management officials at the Houston Police Department told me the higher starting pay and sign-up bonuses were a much more significant factor in boosting recruiting. They pointed to the fact that the city had more than enough candidates to fill the current academy class when the city offered a $5,000 sign-up bonus. That is far less costly than a life-time pension.

And, of course, the reality is that many municipalities and other public entities recruit employees without offering defined benefit plans. For example, the Texas Municipal Retirement System, which covers about 140,000 employees throughout the state, is a money-purchase retirement plan, which is sort of a hybrid between a defined benefit and a defined contribution plan.

Anyone who is proposing pension reform that does not ultimately wean the city off of defined benefit plans is not being serious about solving this problem. Defined benefit plans have been proved time and again to be nothing but a vehicle for elected officials to placate employees by promising them benefits they don't have to worry about paying for. They are a device governmental entities can use to borrow money without going to the voters for approval. Regardless of how meager the benefits are, elected officials will never fully fund them.

But even if we stop digging, that does not fill the $3.7 billion hole we have now.

There are those who advocate changing the retirement system for existing employees. Some have even gone so far as to suggest that we claw back benefits because of some abuses, as I noted in previous columns. Certainly in the private sector, existing employees have frequently been transitioned from defined benefit to defined contribution plans in mid-career.

But even if you believe that the city and the Legislature made bad deals for the taxpayers when they agreed to these plans, they nonetheless were the deals made by our duly elected representatives. If we do not like the deals they are making for us, we should take up the issue at the ballot box. It is not justification for reneging on deals made.

So what do we do about the $3.7 billion hole? We stretch out the payments.

Houston has the great fortune of a strong economy, which—God willing—is likely to continue for some time. We have the luxury of borrowing this money at very low rates and spreading out the shortfall over a longer term. It is not an ideal solution, but if we try to continue making the payments as scheduled, we will either need to significantly raise property taxes or severely cut back city services, and we will not be able to make the infrastructure investments the city will need if it is to continue to grow.

But if the taxpayers are going to step up and bond this indebtedness, I think there are some other issues that should be on the table for negotiations with the city employees. For example, I have always thought it is crazy for pension trustees to be in charge of how the trust funds are invested while the city is on the hook for the investment results. The pension plans continually laud their investment prowess, so it only seems reasonable that they should shoulder the risk of their investment decisions.

I also think employees should have the right to opt out of the pension plans at a discounted cash value. Many city employees have told me they would prefer to have control over their retirement accounts.

Who would oppose a plan to stop offering city employees defined contribution benefits? Taxpayers should favor it because it reduces the pressure for more tax increases or service cuts. Existing employees should favor it because they get what they were promised.

The one group that will not like it is the cottage industry that has developed around these pension plans. Last year, the plans doled out $54 million in salaries to pension plan executives, Wall Street investment bankers, lawyers, lobbyists, accountants and actuaries. They will come up with every reason you can imagine to keep the city on the path to financial ruin so that they can keep their noses in the pension trough.

President Ronald Reagan once said, "There are no easy answers, but there are simple answers. We must have the courage to do what we know is morally right." Continuing to make retirement promises that are not sustainable is not morally right. And it is irresponsible for future taxpayers and future municipal employees.

May 28, 2014

What Drives Medicare Costs?

One of the principal drivers of escalating Medicare costs has been the increased life expectancy of beneficiaries since the program began and the increases in life expectancy that are anticipated in the future.

When Medicare was first adopted in 1965, the average life expectancy for a 65-year-old person was about 14 years. Today, however, the average life expectancy of a 65-year-old is more than 18 years, meaning that the average Medicare beneficiary will be collecting benefits for four years longer than when the program was first implemented. When Medicare was adopted, it was expected that people would be collecting benefits for about 30 percent of the time they were employed and paying Medicare taxes. However, with today's increased life expectancy, they will now be collecting benefits for a period equal to about 40 percent of their working careers.

The cost of these extra years is significant. Today the average annual cost per Medicare beneficiary is about $11,000. Assuming that medical costs only escalate at 4 percent annually (an optimistic projection), the annual cost for a person entering Medicare this year will rise to nearly $25,000 in 18 years. The total cost for that person's benefits during the last 18 years of life will be about $300,000. Had that person died after 14 years, total cost would have been only a little more than $200,000. So adding only four years to the life-expectancy assumption increases the projected cost of Medicare by nearly 50 percent.

Also, in 1965 about 28 percent of the population died before reaching age 65. All of those unfortunate folks paid Medicare taxes into the system but never collected any benefits. With increased life expectancy and lower mortality rates, today only 17 percent of the population does not survive to the age of 65. And with advances in medical and safety technology, these trends are likely to continue. The bottom line is that we are going to have a lot more people on Medicare for a lot longer than was contemplated when the program was adopted if we keep the eligibility age at 65.

And that trend shows no sign of abating. In 2009 about 47 million Americans were enrolled in Medicare. By the middle of this century, that number is projected to more than double.

It is not surprising then that many of the proposals for restructuring Medicare, including the plan put forward by Paul Ryan and the House Republicans, include beginning to gradually increase the eligibility age. Under the Ryan proposal, the eligibility age would stay at 65 until 2020 and then start going up, ultimately reaching 69 and a half.

However, increasing the eligibility age will not save as much as one might think. First, the years being eliminated are those early years in which beneficiaries tend to be healthier and have lower costs.

One study estimated that 26 percent of all Medicare expenses are incurred in the last year of a person's life, a phenomenon that would largely be unaffected by an increase in the eligibility age.

Also, raising the eligibility age might end up costing other government programs more. If we raise the eligibility age to 69 but more seniors 65-69 start showing up at Ben Taub Hospital's emergency room, it is questionable whether we will have saved anything. The bottom line is we probably need to start raising Medicare's eligibility age incrementally, but that will not be the silver bullet that saves Medicare.

July 22, 2011

Few of Us Contribute Enough

M edicare beneficiaries sometimes tell me they are entitled to Medicare benefits because they earned them by contributing to the system for their entire careers. In a purely legal sense that is true, since the law provides that a person qualifies for Medicare if that person has paid Medicare taxes for at least 10 years. However, very few people actually put enough into the Medicare system to pay for their own benefits.

If we take a hypothetical employee who entered the work force in 1965 and retired in 2010, and assume that employee earned the country's median income for his career, that person and his employer would have paid about $23,000 in Medicare taxes by the time the employee retired. If the amount contributed each year had been put into a savings account earning 5 percent interest, there would have been a balance in the employee's account at the end of the employee's career of about $50,000.

But the annual average benefit paid to Medicare participants today is about $11,700. Of that amount, most Medicare beneficiaries pay an annual premium of about $1,200, leaving a net average cost of just over $10,000. So it would take only about five years to exhaust the contributions made by the employee, assuming that those contributions had been placed in a savings account. However, the average life expectancy at age 65 is now 18 years, meaning the money put into the system for our hypothetical employee would run out 13 years before the employee dies.

The federal government currently estimates that after deducting the premiums Medicare beneficiaries pay, the total cost for the average beneficiary for his or her lifetime will be more than $250,000. Even if we discount those future benefits to their current net present value (basically the amount you would need in savings today to pay for the average person's Medicare benefits), the average employee's contributions are still less than one-third of the cost.

Even most of those with higher incomes have not paid in nearly enough to cover their own likely benefits. Until 1993, the total amount of income subject to the Medicare tax (2.9 percent) was capped. The maximum started at $6,600 in 1966 and was increased to $135,000 in 1993. Since 1993, 100 percent of earned income has been subject to Medicare tax.

If a person earned the maximum amounts or more from 1966 to 1993, the total contributions plus interest earned on contributions by 1993 would have been about $35,000. To have enough to cover his own Medicare costs, the employee would have had to have continued earning at least $135,000 annually after 1993 until retirement in 2010. Obviously, only a small percentage of American workers earn this amount of money.

In reality, the situation is even worse than this hypothetical suggests. As mentioned above, a person can qualify after paying as little as 10 years of Medicare taxes, as opposed to the 45 years assumed in the hypothetical. Also, the spouse of a person who qualifies for Medicare also receives benefits even if that spouse never paid any Medicare taxes. And of course many individuals received benefits in the early days of Medicare who had paid little or nothing into the system. Oh, and by the way, almost none of previous contributions were actually put into a savings account, so the system has earned very little interest.

The truth is the vast majority of people who have received

Medicare benefits paid for a small fraction of the cost of those benefits. And the same will be true for those of us who will retire in the next decade or so.

So, if we are not paying for our own health care, who is? Our children.

We can delude ourselves as much as we want that the money is going to come from taxes on millionaires or oil companies or whatever other demagoguery of the moment the Washington politicians may be dishing out. But the plain fact is that we, as a generation, have decided we would rather our children and grandchildren pay for health care than pay for it ourselves.

In some ways, this may not be all that different from the way humans have traditionally cared for their elders. But with increasing life expectancies and ever-expanding medical options for enhancing the quality of life in our latter years, we must face the reality that we are simply asking future generations to shoulder too large of a burden.

So as we face the difficult challenge of how to reform Medicare, it might be salutary to imagine that the person writing the checks to pay for our medical bills is not some faceless, nameless government bureaucrat but rather one of our own children or grandchildren. And then we need to ask ourselves how comfortable we are with that image.

August 7, 2011

Is Single Payer Inevitable?

I recently had the opportunity to hear one of Houston's leading hospital CEOs give a presentation on how medical expenses are paid under our current system, if it can even be called systematic.

After almost two hours, my head was spinning. The acronyms and vernacular were indecipherable. The billing procedures are arcane and have little connection to the reality of the costs. It is not a system that any rational person would design from a blank piece of paper.

Of course, there is a financial cost to this state of disarray. Most studies show that the portion of health care dollars spent on administration in the United States far exceeds that of other countries and is one of the drivers of our outsized health care costs.

Perhaps the most maddening aspect of the system is how the cost of uninsured care, and the cost of Medicare and Medicaid care that is not reimbursed by the government, are shifted over to insured patients.

As a result, you end up with a single Advil costing several dollars and obscene markups on routine procedures as were recently described in *Time* magazine's widely read article "Bitter Pill" by Steven Brill.

There is a lot of discussion about reforming the current system. One such reform that gets a lot of play is paying providers for outcomes instead of procedures. But, for the most part, a patient's care is not restricted or controlled by a single health care provider, so it is difficult to hold a particular provider entirely responsible for the outcome. And of course, an outcome-based system is also complicated by the patient's behavior. If a doctor prescribes the right medicine but the patient does not take it, it is hardly fair to penalize the doctor.

Reform efforts are further complicated by the interplay among the hospitals, the doctors, the pharmacies, the pharmaceutical companies, the insurance companies, the employers and the state and federal government and local public health organizations. Each has very significant financial vested interests in the current system, and many groups benefit from the existing system—as convoluted as it may be.

In almost any reform there will be winners and losers among these players, which means that any potential loser will have legions of lobbyists on Capitol Hill protecting their interests.

As a result, there is incessant infighting among the various stakeholders over how to reform the system. It is almost impossible to imagine all of the players coming together on a reform plan.

I left the hospital CEO's presentation with the sinking feeling that a single-payer system is inevitable.

Exposés like the *Time* article, regardless of whether you consider it an accurate depiction or not, and the oppressive cost burden of the current system are going to drive popular demand toward some kind of reform. Single-payer is a model that has been adopted by most other developed democracies, demonstrating both its popular appeal and, at least, basic systemic viability.

Whether a single-payer system would be better or worse than the current system is far above my pay grade.

As a general proposition, I am reluctant to make dramatic changes to a system that is, despite all its complexities and shortcomings, delivering quality health care in large volumes.

The inevitability of unintended consequences from such sharp diversions is nearly always underestimated and the reason why

I thought the Affordable Care Act was ill-advised.

But regardless of the merits of a single-payer system, it may well become a political inevitability if the health care industry does not get its act together. The American public will put up with horror stories like those described in the *Time* story for only so long.

April 20, 2013

Do Americans Pay Too Much?

One of the principal arguments used by proponents of the Affordable Care Act (ACA) in support of health care reform is that Americans spend far more for care than people in other developed countries but get poorer results. The evidence that we get poorer results is primarily based on a slightly lower life expectancy for Americans than for people in the other developed countries. But there are many reasons why life expectancies vary from country to country.

The fact that the U.S. is spending far more on its health care system than other developed economies cannot be denied. By virtually any measure, the U.S. is an outlier. U.S. health care spending currently stands at around 17 percent of gross domestic product, or about $8,000 per capita. That is almost double the average spent by other developed countries. This outsized spending is one of the biggest drivers of the federal government's deficit in Medicare and Medicaid.

The conclusion drawn by many, and especially by supporters of the ACA, is that this higher cost is evidence of an inefficient delivery system. That may be, but there are other, and I would argue more cogent, reasons why our health care tab is so much higher.

First and foremost is that we generally have an unhealthier lifestyle than most other countries. As I noted last week, the U.S. ranks near the top of the world's list of the most obese countries. All of the developed countries that spend considerably less than we do are far below us on the fat list.

The U.S. also ranks high among the world's countries in the incidence of adult onset diabetes. Diabetes is a disease that is greatly affected by diet and exercise and can lead to a number of very serious and very costly complications. Most other developed countries have about 30 percent to 40 percent fewer diabetics per capita than the U.S.

Another reason our health care cost is so much higher is simply that we consume a great deal more care than other developed countries, especially in procedures that are elective or for conditions that are not life-threatening.

Knee replacements are a good example. In recent years, on average, about a million knee replacements a year are performed worldwide. And although the U.S. makes up only about 5 percent of the world population, more than 50 percent of the knee replacements were performed here. In the U.S. the number of knee replacements is about 200 per 100,000 persons. The average for the European Union and Canada is a little more than 100 per 100,000 persons.

And I will give you one guess which country has more breast augmentations, liposuctions and nose jobs than the rest of the world combined.

Another challenge for the U.S. with respect to overall health care costs is our cultural approach to end of life care. Medicare now estimates that 27 percent of its budget goes for care provided in the last year of life, and a big chunk of that is spent in the last few weeks of a person's life. The Lien Foundation did a study on end of life care in 40 developed countries. While the U.S. ranked high on the availability and quality of end-of-life care, its cost of care was one of the highest.

Many of us as families have faced the question of when to let go of a sick, elderly family member. No one wants to think about whether the cost of providing care should be considered in making these decisions. But the disproportionate cost of providing end-of-life care is a reality, and most of us are unprepared to deal with it.

To the credit of the ACA's proponents, the bill originally contained a provision that would pay doctors to have end-of-life counseling sessions with their patients. However, that provision was dropped when Sarah Palin and some other Republicans shamefully and outrageously demagogued the issue by alleging it set up "death panels." Fortunately since then the Obama administration has begun paying for such sessions under other regulatory authority, but such limited counseling seems unlikely to make much of a dent in this problem.

There is no doubt that our health care costs are on an unsustainable trajectory. The effect the ACA will have on that trajectory is anyone's guess. But I seriously doubt it is going to have much effect on Americans' dietary habits, the incidence of diabetes, our penchant for cosmetic surgery or our cultural choices around end-of-life decisions.

July 25, 2012

Bad Policy, Bad Politics

I have had serious reservations about the Affordable Care Act from the beginning. It is not that I am oblivious to the plight of nearly 50 million of our fellow Americans who do not have health insurance. And it was obvious that something had to be done about folks with pre-existing conditions as well as some of the other acute problems with our health care system.

My problem was that there was no way for anyone to know what effect the more than 2,000 pages of legislation was going to have on an industry that makes up 20 percent of the economy. Unintended consequences of the legislation already are showing up. For example, there are numerous reports of companies cutting their employees' hours to below 30 hours per week to avoid the law, which launched health care insurance exchanges Tuesday.

And the truth remains that no one, including President Barack Obama and Sen. Ted Cruz, R-Texas, has any idea what the full impact of the law will be, positive or negative. Having said all of that, the current push by Republicans to defund the law is bad public policy and bad politics for the GOP.

There is little precedent for Congress to pass a law and then deny the executive branch the funds to enforce it. In many ways, "defunding" an existing statute would exacerbate the uncertainty and confusion over the new law. And there are certain provisions of the law, such as the ban against denying coverage for pre-existing conditions, which are absolutely needed and overwhelmingly supported by the

American people. But the Republican strategy to completely defund the health act would throw the baby out with the bath water.

Politically speaking, Republicans have to accept that elections have consequences. The issue of repealing the Affordable Care Act was fully debated in the last election and the guy who proposed it was re-elected by a broad margin. The Republicans justify their opposition to the act notwithstanding the president's re-election on two grounds:

First, they argue that while Americans returned the president to the White House, they also returned control of the House to Republicans, and, therefore, Americans wanted a split government and exactly this kind of throttle on Obama. The only problem is that a majority of Americans did not want split government. Democrats running for House seats in 2012 got almost 1 million more votes than Republicans running for the House. The only reason the Republicans retained control of the House is because they were able to gerrymander seats in their favor after the 2000 census when Republicans got control of many state houses.

Republicans also argue that the polls show a majority of Americans are opposed to the implementation of the Affordable Care Act. Most polls show something in the high 50s opposed to the law. The only problem is that the same polls show that about 20 percent of those who oppose the act do so because it did not go far enough. Rather than returning to the previous system, they want a single-payer system.

Whatever reservations the voters may have with the Affordable Care Act, Republicans have not made the case with a majority of Americans to go back to what we had before the new law.

Finally, the Republican attempt to defund the act, and especially using the threat of a government shutdown to do so, is political suicide. Polls show that overwhelming majorities of Americans are opposed to the tactic. In fact, the only group that thinks it is a good idea are those who identify themselves as supporters of the tea party, and then by only about 56 percent. But here is the real irony. Going into the mid-term elections, the president's popularity has been gradually but steadily declining. The rollout of the health care act has been having problems and false starts, giving the Republicans plenty of campaign fodder for 2014 on that issue. It certainly was beginning to appear that the Republicans could have a decent mid-term election as has traditionally been the case for the party not occupying the White House.

But with the current antics, it now appears more likely that the Republicans have snatched defeat from the jaws of victory. Here is the message that Republicans need to hear loud and clear: If you want to repeal the Affordable Care Act, go win an election.

October 2, 2013

Personal Responsibility Has Limits

P art of the conservatives' mantra about health care in the United States is that there should be a greater emphasis on personal responsibility. The theory goes that if individuals bear the consequences of their health choices, such as the decision to smoke, they will make better choices. As a result, the costs of health care will come down generally, and those who make better choices will not be shouldering the costs for those who did not.

The theory is hard to argue with. But in the real world, it runs up against daunting problems.

Generally, people get really sick from one of three things. First, there are those seemingly random diseases that we cannot associate with the victim's behavior—a child struck with cancer, for instance. Increasingly, we are learning that susceptibility to many of these diseases may be pre-programmed in our genes. For people in this category, individual responsibility is a meaningless concept.

One could argue that personal responsibility for such eventualities would be to have catastrophic insurance. However, many young families simply cannot afford that kind of insurance, and many others suffer from pre-existing conditions that, prior to the Affordable Care Act, would have prevented them from getting insurance.

Second, people get sick because of poor lifestyle choices. Smoking and overeating are the two most prevalent of these. Ideally, people who smoke should be "assessed" the cost of their care. However, a person who has gotten lung cancer from smoking will likely show up at a charity or public hospital's emergency room one day. At that point, if we are going to really enforce personal responsibility, we should say, "Sorry, if you cannot afford to be treated, you just need to go away and die." Even if you think that is what should happen, it is not going to in this country.

Instead of paying for his or her care, that person will be absorbed by county hospital district taxes, insurance premiums and charitable gifts. Like it or not, we all are going to bear a large portion of the costs of people's poor lifestyle choices.

And we have to face reality when it comes to addiction. The abuse of drugs—and here I am including nicotine and alcohol—adds tremendously to our health care costs. And if we think we are going to solve addiction by making addicts take personal responsibility for their actions, we are kidding ourselves.

The third reason people get sick is because they get old.

Now, it is unquestionably true that if you live a healthier life, you likely will have fewer health care needs in later years. But experts estimate that 20 percent to 30 percent of a person's lifetime medical expenses will come in the last year of his or her life.

So who is up for telling people in the last year of their lives that they need to take more personal responsibility for their health care costs?

And then there is the issue of mental illness. It adds to our health care costs both directly, through the treatment of mental illnesses, and indirectly, because it is related to many physical ailments as well.

Ken Maddox, the longtime head of Ben Taub Hospital, once told me that roughly 30 percent of their emergency room visits were individuals with mental illness who had injured themselves or someone else. I do not think we are going to get very far trying to explain personal responsibility to a schizophrenic.

Ideals and principles are important guides for public policy. But in health care, as is frequently the case, it turns out even well-intentioned ideology does us little good in addressing real-world problems.

Certainly, injecting personal responsibility into the health care system anywhere it's practical is a good idea. But to believe that we can just stand back and let an ideal like personal responsibility work some kind of magic on a problem as complex as our current health care conundrum is nonsense.

April 23, 2014

Lessons From Canada

I often hear commentators warn that our health care system is becoming like Canada's, as if that were a horrible evil to be avoided at all costs. I have been traveling in Canada for the past couple of weeks. I took the occasion to conduct my own highly unscientific poll about what Canadians think about their health care system.

Canada has an extensive single-payer system, where the government is essentially the insurer for all basic health care. In some ways, it is like Medicare except it covers everyone, not just those older than 65.

All health care that is considered essential is provided to the patient for free. The costs are financed primarily through income taxes, so their tax rates are considerably higher than ours. There is a private market for nonessential medical service, such as elective cosmetic surgery. About 30 percent of all health care services are delivered by this private market.

According to the World Bank, Canada spends about 11 percent of its gross domestic product on health care. That compares to just under 18 percent for the U.S. By the roughest crude measurements of health care, life expectancy and infant mortality, Canada bests us by a bit.

Of course, it is always difficult to compare the cost effectiveness of two countries' health care systems. There are thousands of other variables, other than the kind of payment system used, that affect costs and outcomes. It would be misleading to make too great of a comparison between a small country like Canada and one as large as the United States.

However, what the users think about the system and the degree to which they are satisfied or dissatisfied is a relevant indicator. If you look at the polling, Canadians are significantly more satisfied with their health care system than we are. Most polls show that they support their system by 70-80 percent margins. They also, by an overwhelming majority, say they prefer their system to the system in the United States.

So against this backdrop, I conducted my survey of Canadians I ran across during my trip. As I suppose is human nature, most of the maple-leafers I talked to started out complaining about their system. There are apparently significant wait times to see a doctor for anything that is not critical. There is also some lack of choice regarding providers. And no one like the taxes they have to pay.

But when I asked if they would prefer to change their system to be more like ours, there was a resounding, "No." They found the idea that you could end up uninsured merely because you had been laid off to be a travesty. And while they don't like paying as much in taxes as they do, they seemed to think the security of knowing health care is available was worth the trade-off.

Mostly, the conversations underscored to me that there is no perfect health care system. And I think that is important to remember as we move forward. It is clear that we are not going to stay in the status quo, and we are not going back to the system we had before the Affordable Care Act. Increasingly, the polling is showing that Americans are opposed to repealing the law but at the same time are not at all satisfied with it in its current state.

So the system is going to evolve. But what we are lacking is any kind of overarching policy goals or framework to direct that evolution. Sure, we would all like to not be spending nearly 18 percent of our GDP on health care. But we are not willing to do any of the hard things, such as talking more openly about end-of-life medical care—for instance, use of health-care directives. In practice, these more often than not direct against "heroic" and costly medical care.

Unfortunately, President Barack Obama squandered his considerable political capital when elected by expending it on a hodge-podge attempt to reform health insurance instead of trying to restructure the health care delivery system. He also failed to engage the American people in a candid conversation about the choices we face or to develop a national consensus on health care policy.

Republicans have been even worse on the issue, spending their time fear mongering about the Affordable Care Act, *a la* the death panel demagoguery to score political points. They are also bankrupt when it comes to ideas about alternative solutions. Selling health insurance across state lines and national medical tort reform might be good ideas, but they are hardly the answer to our national health care dilemma.

Perhaps a presidential candidate will emerge in the 2016 campaign who can lead the country in this discussion. The Canadians did so in the 1980s, and they came up with a system that is supported by a wide majority of their citizens. While their system probably would not work for us, they, at least, had the national conversation and came to a consensus. We need to do the same.

June 4, 2014

Hard But Necessary Conversation

I am losing a longtime friend to cancer. It is a heart-breaking experience through which many others have suffered as well.

He is being treated by one of Houston's great hospitals,
which means he's being treated by one the world's great hospitals.
But he is losing the battle nonetheless and likely will not be with us
much longer.

The experience has underscored three thoughts for me.

The first is how fortunate those of us who enjoy good health
are and how easily we take our health for granted. You only need to
spend a short time in the cancer ward of one of our hospitals to be
reminded that you really don't have any problems in your life.

I have also been reminded of the limits to even today's medical technology. This great institution and the great doctors and staff
who work there have thrown all their skill and knowledge at this mi-
croscopic malignancy, but it has still defeated them. You can read in
their faces the frustration at their helplessness, knowing of the disease's advance.

But the most significant takeaway has been the mind-numbing
complexity of trying to navigate our health care system—a hurdle
faced by anyone with a serious illness.

First, there is just trying to understand the medical issues. As
our knowledge of the human body has advanced, the scope of the
information available has increased exponentially. And given the
fact that medical personnel frequently speak in a vernacular alien to

most of us, it is almost impossible just to understand what is going on medically and make a judgment as to what kind of treatment is most appropriate.

Determining what kind of treatment someone needs is just the beginning. In many ways, what has been worse in my experience is trying to figure out what care is available from which source, and then determining how it will be paid for.

My friend is on Medicare and has private insurance. Once we had some handle on the kind of care he needed, his family and I spent hours trying to figure if either would pay for all or part of his treatment.

And it is so difficult to get a definitive answer. You'll hear a lot of hedging, and when you do get an answer from a government or insurance representative, about half the time the next person tells you something completely different.

From my experience it is not from a lack of people wanting to be helpful. To the contrary, most of the workers in the health care and medical insurance industries I have encountered have gone out of their way to try and help. But the complexity of the system overwhelms even those who work with it on a daily basis.

All of these issues are made more difficult when dealing with an end-of-life situation where no planning has been done ahead of time. We are so loath to discuss our own mortality or that of our loved ones. Yet it is one of the few certainties we will all face. From this experience I would say, overall, we do a pretty lousy job of dealing with it.

I recently talked to an anesthesiologist who had lost his wife to a long, painful battle with cancer. He recounted with great sadness and a pain that had barely faded with time how she had unnecessarily suffered long past when there was any hope of a recovery. He told me that in his opinion we treat our pets more humanely at the end of their lives than we do our families.

These are the toughest issues any of us will ever face. I don't pretend to have the answers. What I do know is that people facing serious illness are in for a nightmare with the current maze of insurance, government programs and multiple institutions and service providers that largely work in silos. It is an unconscionable burden on individuals and families already facing difficult times. The structures also are highly inefficient and enormously costly, and this should concern us, whether we're ratepayers or taxpayers. There are redundancies and gaps in this byzantine system, extremes that can prevent even those with financial resources from getting the best care.

We are, notwithstanding that it is an unpleasant and scary subject, going to have to conduct a national conversation about end-of-life care. We are going to have to decide what level of basic care we are going to guarantee to every American, and how to pay for it. We are going to have to create serious disincentives for those who engage in unhealthy and risky behavior. If you are going to smoke or eat yourself into oblivion, the rest of us should not have to pay for it.

Of course, all of this is easier said than done. But we have got to be able to do better than the current quagmire.

June 12, 2014

Drilling Down
on Income Disparity

P sychologists have long known that people with below-average IQs tend to overestimate their IQ while people with higher-than-average IQs tend to underestimate theirs. The pattern is part of a larger phenomenon known as illusory superiority, where most people will rank themselves a little above average with respect to favorable attributes. The same is true when we are asked about our relative incomes.

According to the most recent statistics from the IRS, you need to make about $340,000 annually to be in the top 1 percent of annual household incomes. But it only takes $112,000 to make it into the top 10 percent. The 50 percent cut-off is $32,000. That is to say, half the households in the U.S. take in less than $32,000 per year. The U.S. Census Bureau has slightly higher numbers primarily because the agency's data includes some nontaxable income. According to the Census Bureau, the median income in the U.S. is around $50,000. The middle 20 percent of incomes range from $38,000 to $62,000.

Meanwhile, 20 percent of households earn less than $20,000 annually and 20 percent, more than $100,000.

But consistent with what psychologists find with respect to other attributes, both high and low income-earners tend to see themselves as middle-class. In a recent Wall Street Journal/NBC poll, a plurality of every income category up to $100,000 thought they were a middle-class income. Interestingly, though, 52 percent of those polled believed the middle income was something between $40,000 and $75,000, which actually is quite accurate. Those who tended to be the most inaccurate in their estimates were those with higher incomes.

If you were to look at a bell curve of income distributions for the U.S., it would be significantly shifted to the left as there are significantly more low income-earners than high ones. What most studies did find, and what worries many observers, is that the curve appears to have shifted significantly more to the left over the past several decades.

But even more worrisome to some is that the effect is greatly exaggerated at the extreme high-income levels. Depending on what data you use, the top 10 percent of income-earners draw somewhere between 40 percent and 50 percent of all pre-tax income. Thirty years ago, the top 10 percent's share was closer to 30 percent. Regardless of your political views or explanations for this disparity, it is hard to argue this is a good thing for the country. Many of those on the left attribute this disparity to government policy, especially what they view as "tax loopholes" for the rich. However, this is not likely the cause.

First, regardless of various specific exemptions and deductions, we nonetheless have a very progressive income-tax structure. Currently, the top 10 percent of income-earners pay more than 70 percent of all income taxes. Those earning less than the median income (for tax purposes, about $32,000) pay only about 2 percent of all income taxes. Currently, about half of all households pay no federal income tax. To be fair, those who do not pay income tax do pay payroll taxes, as do their employers on their behalf. However, the payroll taxes go to fund Social Security and Medicare, entitlements on which virtually all of those households will one day rely. So those Americans are making no contribution to the balance of the cost of maintaining the federal government's other functions, such as our defense.

Also, most of the so-called tax loopholes actually benefit the middle class, at least in terms of the amount of tax saved. The 10 largest exemptions or deductions in terms of the amount of tax saved are personal, not corporate. The two largest are not having to pay taxes on the money your employer spends on your health insurance and the home mortgage deduction. And both of these are already limited on the high end.

The truth is that the recent trend toward greater income disparity is a complex phenomenon, likely rooted in numerous causes. There is undoubtedly some work that needs to be done on the tax code to eliminate some of the more egregious benefits to some individuals and corporations. But those who think they are going to solve this problem with the tax code are kidding themselves.

December 14, 2013

Real Reason for Rising Unemployment

S ince the 2008 recession began, we have been unable to bring down the unemployment rate. In the ramp-up to the 2012 campaign, both parties have been hammering away that the policies of the other are to blame. Both have harkened back to the golden days, respectively of Reagan or Clinton, as evidence that their policies will solve the unemployment problem.

But neither party acknowledges that unemployment generally has been getting worse in the U.S. for decades, through both Republican and Democratic administrations and congresses. Since 1950 the unemployment rate has ranged from 2.5 percent to more than 10 percent. But there is an unmistakable trend upward. Since 1950, there have been 10 peaks and nine bottoms in the unemployment rate. With the exception of the period from about 1990 to 2005, every peak and bottom has been higher than the previous one. For the mathematicians among you, the trend line for the unemployment rate from 1950 to today has a statistically positive slope. Unemployment on average has been getting worse by about .03 percent each year or by about 1 percent over each 30-year period.

So if unemployment has been getting worse for the last 60 years, including periods when both parties were in power, it would seem to raise the question whether there is a cause for it other than the ideological hogwash to which we are constantly subjected by both parties.

The answer is no mystery. Anyone who has been an employer

for the last several decades, as I have been, can provide the answer. Our tax and regulatory policies have increasingly discouraged hiring more employees.

There are two decisions that any employer faces when considering whether to add an employee. The threshold question is whether the employer needs additional help. Notwithstanding that some liberals seem to feel that businesses have an obligation to hire people whether they need them or not, employers are simply not going to hire additional employees unless they need the extra help to create the goods and services demanded by their customers.

In this regard, Democrats are correct that employment, at least over the short term, is driven by demand. The ebb and flow of the demand for goods and services in the business cycle is what accounts for the significant short-term variations in the unemployment rate. If you believe that government policy can stimulate demand, a proposition that many are justifiably skeptical of, the Democrats' argument for more stimulus is at least logically consistent. But even if the Democrats are right about additional stimulus reducing the unemployment rate, that is clearly a short-term phenomenon and cannot explain why unemployment has gotten consistently worse over the last 60 years.

The long-term cause, I believe, has to do with the second consideration most employers face when they need to add additional capacity. That question frequently is: Do I need an employee to do this job or can I automate it? And that question is normally going to turn on the relative costs of hiring an additional employee versus the cost of making an investment in equipment that can do the job or at least allow it to be done with less labor.

And let's face it, automation has some built-in advantages. Machines do not get tired or sick. They don't have family or substance-abuse problems. They don't come to work in a bad mood or fight fellow machines. They are, for the most part, easier to manage.

But we have significantly added to this advantage by handicapping labor with a whole variety of tax and regulatory weights that make it even more attractive to business to invest in equipment instead of people. Any market as complex as the labor market has innumerable factors affecting it. But the fact that we have made it increasingly less attractive to hire new employees for the last 60 years must be one of the most significant factors contributing to the long-term rise in unemployment.

October 3, 2012

Unemployment: A Graying Problem

Historically, unemployment has mostly been a problem people encounter when they are young. Prior to the 2008 recession, those in the 16-to-24 age category have made up about 40 percent of the total number of unemployed. Conversely, those older than 45 have generally had much lower rates of unemployment. The U.S. Bureau of Labor Statistics started breaking out over-45 unemployment in 1976. Through the 1980s, there were, on average, just more than 1 million individuals older than 45, and they made up only about 17 percent of all unemployed.

But beginning around 2000, unemployment in the over-45 cohort began to rise. By 2002 for the first time more than 2 million Americans older than 45 were unemployed, and they made up an unprecedented 25 percent of the unemployed. In 2005 to 2007 the number of over-45 unemployed dipped below 2 million but continued to rise as a percentage of all unemployed.

During the Great Recession, however, over-45 unemployment exploded. The number of over-45 unemployed nearly tripled from about 1.8 million in late 2007 to nearly 5.2 million by early 2010. By that time, over-45s made up more than one-third of all unemployed Americans.

The recovery has helped over-45s less than other age groups. In every other age category, there are fewer unemployed today than at the end of 1990-1991 recession. However, at the end of that recession, there were only about 1.8 million over-45s who were unemployed. Today, there are nearly double that number.

The over-45 unemployed are also whiter than the unemployed generally. While whites make up only about 60 percent of all unemployed, they make up 75 percent of the over-45 unemployed. The over-45s also make up the largest segment of the long-term unemployed.

These changing employment patterns have a number of policy implications.

First, they would seem to suggest that there is some kind of structural employment problem. It may be something as simple as technology changing faster than our ability to retrain older workers. The offshoring of many midlevel positions probably also contributed to the problem. But it certainly puts into question whether indirect policies such as fiscal or monetary stimulus will do anything to address the problem of older Americans being unemployed.

There are also many cost implications. The most obvious is unemployment insurance. The federal government's outlays for unemployment benefits nearly quadrupled from $40 billion annually to nearly $160 billion in the wake of the Great Recession. That has subsided some since the emergency benefits expired, but the Congressional Budget Office projects the cost of the program to continue at an elevated level indefinitely.

There are also indirect costs. The fastest-growing segment of Medicaid beneficiaries are adults under 65. From 2000 to 2010 the number of those jumped from just more than 5 million to 11.3 million. They now account for about 20 percent of all Medicaid beneficiaries and, other than children, are the largest single group of beneficiaries. I cannot help thinking that a lot of these folks are some of those unemployed who lost their group health insurance and cannot afford to buy private insurance because they are out of work.

Unfortunately, while the problems of the older, long-term

unemployed can be readily identified, the solutions are more elusive. Everyone talks about retraining programs, but there is no evidence that such programs have had much impact.

Ironically, the increase in more older people being unemployed came after the Age Discrimination in Employment Act of 1967, demonstrating that it is easier to outlaw discrimination than it is to actually end it.

Perhaps the more serious question is whether this surge in older Americans being unemployed is just a temporary side effect of the Great Recession or whether there is some more permanent, structural change in the labor market that will perpetuate this problem into the future.

Hopefully some good social scientists and economists will take on trying to get to the bottom of this phenomenon. Otherwise it is going to continue to be a costly problem, both in financial and human terms, a problem our economy can't afford.

April 30, 2014

Give Thanks for Being Born Here

I get the most feedback from readers when I write about immigration. Much of it is passionate. Most of it is belligerent to those here illegally. There are two things I hear almost invariably from those who oppose immigration reform, both of which are wrong, and there is one thing I never hear.

The first thing I always hear is that those here illegally are criminals and have no rights. Of course, criminals actually have rights, as do noncitizens, under our legal system. But laying that misstatement of the law aside, it is also inaccurate to say that every one of the 10 million or so living here without a visa has committed a crime. About 40 percent came here on a valid visa that has now expired. Overstaying a visa subjects that person to deportation; however, it is not a crime. About another 20 percent were brought here as children and therefore are not legally responsible for entering the country without a visa.

As for the 40 percent who did break the law by crossing the border without permission, they have committed only a misdemeanor punishable by a small fine. Relatively speaking, it is a far less serious crime than say burglary, which is a felony. Given that our police solve only about 12 percent of the burglaries committed, I have a hard time getting worked up about the government not prosecuting every person who has left some hellhole in Central America and walked hundreds of miles to get into this country to make a better life.

The second thing I almost always hear is that those of us

advocating for immigration reform want an "open border" policy with no restrictions on immigration.

To the contrary, we just think that the current system is dumb and ineffective and want a better one.

The principal reason the current system does not work is because it ignores economic reality. If you have a ready supply of inexpensive labor on one side of the border and a demand for it on the other side of the border, the supply is going to meet the demand no matter what the law says. No man-made law is ever going to repeal the law of supply and demand. And no system that ignores fundamental economic realities can ever be effectively enforced over a long period. The Soviet Union could not enforce a border that ran only 87 miles long across Berlin with unlimited resources and no ethical or humanitarian restraints. What are the chances we are going to close a nearly 2,000-mile border?

The great genius of America is that we are the first country in the world based not on geography or tribal affiliation or ethnicity but on principles and ideals. Those ideals—individual liberty, democracy, equality under the law and the guarantee of inalienable rights—are the beacons that have drawn millions to our shores. And it has been the passion of those new immigrant patriots that has kept our national spirit renewed and vital.

My housekeeper became a citizen earlier this year. The day that she voted she brought me her receipt from the electronic voting machine, holding it as if it was her most treasured possession. The idea that she would have passed up the right to vote after waiting so many years to become a citizen never crossed her mind. Yet how many millions of citizens born in this country do not even bother to vote?

That brings me to what I almost never hear from those who have such antipathy for illegal immigrants: any appreciation for how lucky they are to have been born in this country. I do not hear in their voices the sheer joy of being an American citizen that beamed from my housekeeper's face as she proudly showed me her voting receipt that day.

Let's face it, the only real difference between them and us is that we were born here. Those of us who were fortunate enough to be born here were given an incredible birthright. We did not have to earn it as my housekeeper did.

So what I plan to do on this day of thanks giving is to remind myself just how lucky I am to have been born in the most remarkable and unique country in the history of the world and thank the good Lord for that blessing. It is something we should all probably do and do more often than once a year on Thanksgiving.

November 21, 2012

Sanctuary Is Not a Dirty Word

A few weeks ago I attended the gala for the National Holocaust Museum in Washington, D.C. It is not an event I have attended before, but my friend Fred Zeidman was being honored for his service as its chair, and my wife Melissa and I wanted to be part of the Houston contingent that celebrated with him. This year the museum was commemorating the 65th anniversary of the liberation of the concentration camps. More than 100 World War II veterans who participated in the liberation attended the event.

As you might imagine, dozens of spellbinding and inspiring stories were told. However, it was the testimony of one woman I found particularly poignant and prescient for our times. Her name was Magit Meisner. In 1938 she was 16 years old, living with her family in Prague. Fearful of the impending Nazi occupation of Czechoslovakia, her family fled to Paris. So began nearly two years of hopscotching across Europe, always just one step ahead of the advancing Nazi army. They eventually made their way to Portugal and secured passage on a freighter bound for New York.

During their two-year ordeal, they endured many hardships and numerous narrow escapes. Meisner said there was one hope that kept them going, the hope of America. It was the one place in a world gone mad where they knew they would be safe, where they would not be persecuted for their religious beliefs, the one place they would find sanctuary. Meisner choked back tears as she told of reaching America, of her love for this country and of her profound gratitude that God had provided a sanctuary for her and her family.

Today, the word sanctuary has acquired a negative connotation in some quarters. The term "sanctuary city" now evokes derision. How did the incredibly noble idea of America being a place where people could come from all over the world to find freedom and a better life become a bad thing, capable of evoking such vitriol?

Of course, the plight of today's immigrants can hardly be compared to the experiences of Jews fleeing Nazi Germany during World War II. Their circumstances are nowhere near as dire. But it's not difficult to imagine that a young man in a village in El Salvador who is told he must join a gang or be killed might feel threatened and hopeless. And who can blame a father who believes his children will live out their lives with no hope or opportunity for seeking a better life here? I doubt his feelings are much different from many of our forefathers'.

I also find it hard to understand the scorn heaped on young women stealing into the United States to give birth to their children here. "Anchor babies," they are called. What greater measure of faith and belief in this country could a young woman demonstrate than running the gantlet of deserts, outlaw "coyotes" and hundreds of miles of travel just so her child can be born as an American? Which one of us would want anything less for our own children?

It is particularly troubling to me as a Christian that so many of my faith have joined in the anti-sanctuary hysteria. After all, the founder of our faith was forced to flee to Egypt as a refugee when he was an infant. Fortunately for us, the Egyptians had not constructed a fence to keep the riff-raff from Canaan out of their country.

In 1974 Ronald Reagan gave a now iconic speech known as the "Shining City on a Hill" speech. It was a time of great national self-doubt, and Reagan used the speech to remind Americans of the greatness of our country. In what I find to be the most moving part of the speech, Reagan recounts an incident in 1853 involving a U.S. Navy captain named Duncan Ingraham and a Hungarian immigrant named Martin Koszto. Shortly before this incident, Koszto had immigrated to the United States, fleeing from political persecution in the Austrian Empire. He had applied to become a citizen but had not completed the process.

Ingraham was commanding a single American sloop in the port of Smyrna, Turkey. While visiting Smyrna on business, Koszto had been kidnapped by Austrian agents and taken prisoner aboard an Austrian warship in the harbor.

One of Koszto's friends saw the American flag flying from Ingraham's ship and asked for his help. Ingraham went aboard the Austrian warship and demanded to see the prisoner. When Koszto was brought before him, Ingraham asked him a single question. "Are you seeking the protection of the American flag?" When Koszto replied yes, Ingraham gave the Austrian captain until 4 p.m. to release his fellow countryman.

Just before 4 p.m., notwithstanding that the Austrian ship was much larger than Ingraham's and that there were three other Austrian warships in the harbor, Ingraham ordered his ship's cannons rolled out and prepared to fire a broadside into the Austrian ship.

Just then, a small boat was lowered from the Austrian warship, and Koszto rowed with all his might to his country's ship. Ever since this incident, the U.S. Navy has honored Ingraham's heroism with a ship named for him.

What has always made this country unique is its ability to take people from every corner of the globe, speaking every language, practicing every religion, and of every creed, color and heritage and turn them into Americans. But it is not that we homogenize people. We do not require that you give up your heritage to become an American. We relish the fact that we are a hyphenated family, but all having the same last name—American. And we are able to do this because America, like no other country on the planet, was founded on and exists on the shared ideal of freedom.

There are those who will argue that this view is quaint and not sufficiently sophisticated for the complex world in which we live. Some will say that we fight wars today not to free the world but for oil reserves and that we have lost our way and eroded our own civil liberties.

But the people of the world are a strong rebuttal to these critiques as each day they vote with their feet by the millions, desperately trying to reach our shores. Notwithstanding what our detractors may say about our shortcomings, the last time I checked there were no waiting lines to get into Iran or North Korea.

Today, as we wrestle with how our immigration laws should be reformed, and they most certainly must be reformed, it is essential that America does not cease to be the beacon of hope and freedom for the Meisners and the Kosztos of the world.

We must never stop being the country that harkens to the rest of the world to "give us your poor and huddled masses longing to be free." We have, from our beginning, been a sanctuary to the rest of the word. It is what makes America great. It is what makes America, in the words of Ronald Reagan, "the last best hope of man on Earth."

May 23, 2010

Yogi Berra Immigration Plan

O ne of Yogi Berra's many memorable quotes was that "good pitching always beats good hitting . . . or vice versa." His point, of course, was that a successful ball team needed both. Today, the immigration debate is locked between two camps, one screaming for immigration reform and the other for border security. The reform proponents downplay the importance of border security and the border security proponents insist that the border be secured before comprehensive reform can be considered. Both are right, and both are wrong.

It is futile to discuss the immigration issue without putting it into its economic context. We have experienced a large number of immigrants, especially from Latin America, coming to this country without visas over the last two decades because of an economic reality: There was a demand for their labor but no legal mechanism to accommodate that demand.

Those who claim that those came here without a visa "cut in line" and could have come here legally are either disingenuous or not familiar with current immigration law. When we last comprehensively overhauled the immigration system in 1986, the law set the quota for unskilled or semi-skilled workers at 5,000 annually. That means that from 1986 until today, only 125,000 unskilled or semi-skilled workers could have entered the country legally. During this period our economy created jobs for millions.

And it is not the case that these immigrants displaced American workers. During most of this period the unemployment rate was below 6 percent, and at the height of the immigration influx in the early 2000s it dropped below 4 percent, a rate economists consider full employment. Not surprisingly, indications are that the rate of illegal immigration has declined significantly since the onset of the current recession. Unless we have an immigration system that reflects ongoing contemporary economic realities, it is doomed to fail. If we continue to create the lure of jobs but no way for individuals to legally migrate here for those jobs, no amount of resources can secure the border, nor will there be the political will to do so.

However, merely allowing a rational level of immigration (both permanent and temporary) without seriously enforcing our immigration laws would similarly be self-defeating. The border security proponents are correct that we cannot have the rule of law in every other aspect of our society but continue to wink at our immigration laws. And they fairly point out that the last round of immigration reform that did not secure the border, resulting in the current tidal wave of illegal immigration.

At the same time, if we have a rational system that allows for a level of immigration consistent with the demand for labor, there will be less incentive to immigrate illegally and thus make it far easier to secure the border. The obvious solution is to pursue reform of the immigration system and border security simultaneously.

Two political realities, however, are keeping this from happening. First, border security proponents are justifiably suspicious that if immigration reform is adopted, promises to secure the border will not be kept. After all, this was what occurred after the 1986 reform. Immigration reform must be, therefore, tied in ironclad terms to real enforcement measures.

The second political problem is more difficult. Politicians on both sides of the debate believe they benefit politically from the current conundrum. Democrats are pushing immigration reform to pinch Republicans between their conservative base and a growing Hispanic electorate. Republicans, on the other hand, pander to the primary electorate base by seeing who can be the most extreme anti-illegal-immigrant zealot.

Ironically, polls show that the vast majority of Americans seem to have already reached the conclusion that we need both comprehensive reform and enhanced border security. A recent poll showed that over 80 percent of Americans favored *both* creating a legal status for immigrants already living here (if they had a job and no criminal record) *and* spending more money to secure the border. In other words, we need more pitching and more hitting. Now, we just need a manager who will put both on the field.

August 11, 2010

Mass Deportation No Option

W e all know there are about 11 million people living in this country illegally. Virtually all of us agree this is a significant problem. What we cannot seem to agree on is what to do about it. The alternatives are limited. There are basically only three. One, we can do nothing. Two, we can create some kind of status that allows them to live here legally. Three, we can deport all of them. Since no one seems to accept doing nothing (though that is basically what we have done for the last decade), we are left with either creating a legal status or deportation. So what are the practicalities of a mass deportation?

Let's start with the cost. According to the Department of Homeland Security, in 2010 it spent roughly $9.2 billion to deport 392,000 individuals. That comes out to about $23,500 per person. Assuming the cost of rounding up 11 million is scalable (almost certainly not the case), it would cost about $263 billion to deport all illegal immigrants. That is about twice what we are currently spending annually on the war in Afghanistan. In actuality, the cost would be much higher because trying to ramp up to arrest and deport 11 million in a short time would be enormously more difficult. A large number of current deportations are people caught in the act of crossing the border illegally and thus can be returned at a relatively low cost. Rooting someone out of Spanish Harlem and transporting them from New York back to Mexico is going to be much more expensive.

Another significant challenge would be where to put those

detained. Many believe that as soon as a person is arrested for being in the country illegally he or she is immediately shipped off to the border. However, that is only the case if the person is caught in the act of crossing the border illegally. In any other case, there is no way to immediately prove definitely if the person is in the country illegally. We do not carry any national citizenship ID papers, at least not yet. Also, because 40 percent of illegal immigrants came here on a valid visa, there is a question in each of those cases as to whether the visa has been or can be extended.

As a result, a person arrested on suspicion of being here illegally must be detained until a hearing can be held to confirm status. The current waiting time for a hearing is about 36 days. That time will, of course, skyrocket with 11 million deportations. To accomplish this in a year, we would need to arrest about 1 million illegal immigrants each month. If the delay in hearings got to, say, 90 days, we would need detention facilities for about 3 million people. The entire U.S prison population (including all federal, state and local institutions) is only 2.2 million inmates. So trying to figure out how we are going to detain more people than we currently hold in all of the jails and prisons in the country will be quite a challenge.

Then consider the personnel needed to track down 11 million illegal immigrants. Last year, it took about 20,000 Immigration and Customs Enforcement officers to deport 392,000 immigrants. Again, assuming we could maintain that ratio (a grossly optimistic assumption), it would take 571,000 officers to do the job in a year. That is more than we currently have on active duty with the U.S. Army. Probably a better comparison is that it took about 950,000 law enforcement officers nationwide to make about 13 million arrests for all crimes in 2009. Then, of course, there would be the legion of administrative law judges, immigration lawyers, court reporters and ancillary personnel required.

Of course, none of this will ever happen. Even if the country were willing to embark on such a massive undertaking, there would be a wave of civil disobedience and resistance that would render the task impossible. The churches, across nearly all denominations and faiths, are adamantly opposed to mass deportations and would likely offer sanctuary to illegal immigrants. Does anyone think we are really going to send the National Guard into churches to drag women and children out, screaming and crying, and throw them into paddy wagons? Just think of the national angst caused by extracting just one child in the Elian Gonzalez case.

The truth is we have two alternatives. Do nothing or come up with a plan to create a legal status for these folks. The longer we continue to do nothing or cling to the fantasy that we are going to deport 11 million people the worse the problem will get.

February 16, 2011

What Amnesty Doesn't Mean

Maybe it is just the lawyer in me, but I get irritated when I hear people misuse terms, and especially legal terms, to bolster their argument. My current gripe is the way immigration hawks have invented a new meaning for the word amnesty. Amnesty has now become code for any approach to dealing with immigrants living in the country without a valid visa short of deportation.

According to Black's Law Dictionary, an amnesty is "pardon for past acts, granted by government to persons guilty of crime." Amnesty is an act of grace for a person who has committed a crime that relieves that person of the legal guilt and consequences of the crime. The word is misused in the immigration debate in two ways.

First, amnesty implies a complete forgiveness for an offense. In the recent debates over immigration reform, not one serious person has proposed complete forgiveness. Every proposal that Congress has seriously considered over the last decade has included substantial penalties in exchange for the illegal immigrant being granted permission to stay in the United States. Changing the penalty to be imposed for a violation of a law is not amnesty.

Second, for a person to be granted an amnesty, that person must be guilty of committing a crime. Immigration hawks widely believe, or would like for us to believe, that any foreign national living in this country without a valid visa has committed a crime. However, that is not the case. In fact, the overwhelming majority have not, at least, committed a federal immigration crime. Or if they have, they are likely already exempt from prosecution.

The Department of Homeland Security estimates that as of 2009 there were slightly fewer than 11 million foreign nationals living in the United States without valid visas. It surprised me to learn that 3 million to 4 million of these individuals came to the U.S. on a valid visa but have overstayed the time permitted in their visa.

However, overstaying a valid visa is not a crime under federal law. It does subject a person to being detained and deported; however, there is no penalty, such as a fine or jail term.

A person who enters the country without a visa does commit a crime. A statute known as 8 USC §1325 makes it a crime to enter the U.S. at a place or time not approved by immigration officials. A first-time offender is subject to a fine and a jail term of up to six months. Subsequent offenses can result in a two-year jail term. A person who enters the country illegally is also subject to a civil fine not to exceed $250.

As a result of this provision, the 6 million to 7 million illegal immigrants who entered the country without a visa committed an offense under 8 USC §1325 when they entered the country and are subject to prosecution under that law, provided they have no valid defense. However, as it turns out, most of them do have a defense.

First, there is the statute of limitations. Federal law provides that a person cannot be prosecuted after five years. DHS estimates that 90 percent of the illegal immigrant population entered the country prior to 2005. Therefore, the vast majority of illegal immigrants may be subject to deportation, but they cannot be prosecuted under 8 USC §1325 because of the statute of limitations.

Second, many of the foreign nationals who are in the U.S. illegally were brought here as children. Under federal law, a child under the age of 18 cannot, under most circumstances, be prosecuted for a crime. DHS estimates that 1.3 million of the current illegal immigrant population is under the age of 18. Another 1.4 million are between the ages of 18 to 24, and most of these were probably brought here by their parents as minors.

When you add together those who came here legally but overstayed their visa term, those for whom prosecution is barred by limitations and those who crossed the border as children, it is unlikely that more than 1 million of the 11 million illegal immigrants could be prosecuted for a federal immigration crime. That probably explains why the federal government brings only a handful of charges under 8 USC §1325.

So whatever you want to call a procedure by which foreign nationals who are here illegally can apply for permanent residence status and, perhaps ultimately, citizenship, it is clearly not accurate to call it amnesty.

If you are one of those who still believe that the solution to our immigration problem is the deportation of 10 million people, then please just have the guts to admit that is your position and stop debasing the English language by using code words for a policy you are embarrassed to admit you support.

February 8, 2012

What's Really at Issue

I have now sat through editorial political endorsement meetings with nearly a dozen Republican primary candidates. All are eager to talk about immigration, and invariably they begin with "I am opposed to amnesty," followed quickly with "we have to secure the border." On each occasion I have asked the candidate what he or she means by "amnesty." In almost every case the answer has been it means immediately granting illegal immigrants citizenship.

Well, if that is what amnesty means, I am opposed to it, as I suspect is just about everyone else in America.

Several times the candidates tried to tell us the immigration bill passed last year by the U.S. Senate provides for immediate citizenship. Nothing could be further from the truth. About the fastest any immigrant who came here illegally as an adult could become a citizen under the Senate bill is about 13 years. And even to gain that status the immigrant has to meet certain criteria.

The anti-immigration-reform advocates argue that this is such lenient treatment that it will encourage additional waves of illegal immigration. That is nonsense. Just think about it. Some young person in a village in Nicaragua is going to decide to go to America without a visa because immigrants living here now can become citizens after 13 years. Give me a break.

Equally as disingenuous is the tired line that we must "first secure the border." Every time candidates recited that line I asked them what they meant by it. I have yet to hear an answer from which I could discern when the border would actually be secure. In other words, let's put off any kind of immigration reform as long as we can.

Of course, we all know what this real issue is. The Republicans, already in a demographic undertow, are loath to add any voters to the roll that might drag them under even faster. Ironically, the Republican intransigence to immigration reform is doing exactly that.

If the Senate's bill becomes law this year, the first election any of these immigrants could possibly vote in would be the 2028 presidential election. And by the way, if the 1986 immigration reform is any indicator, most of them will never become citizens and thus never vote. A Department of Homeland Security study found that of the roughly 2.7 million immigrants who got green cards as a result of the 1986 law, only about 40 percent ever became citizens.

So let's do the math. Assuming there are about 11 million illegal immigrants here today, and assuming 90 percent apply for and are able to get their green card, that means about 10 million can begin working on their citizenship. If 40 percent become citizens, that means there would be about 4 million potential new registered voters in 2028. Voter turnout on average runs a little over 50 percent. For new citizens it might even be lower. So maybe you have 2 million new actual voters in the 2028 election.

Even as badly as Republicans are currently doing with Latino voters, they are still getting about 30 percent of that vote. So at the end of the day, we might be talking about adding about 1.4 million Democratic votes to 600,000 for Republicans, or a swing of 800,000 votes. McCain lost to Obama by 9 million votes. Romney lost by 5 million votes. It is possible this number of votes could have some impact in a few congressional districts. But at least at the national level, the Democrats' getting 800,000 extra votes in the 2028 presidential election is the least of the Republicans' problems.

Just to put the numbers into even sharper perspective, about

800,000 Latinos are turning 18 each year. The overwhelming majority are already citizens. Nearly 5 million of those who will turn 18 over the next 10 years are citizens already and have, at least, one parent who is living here illegally. So the Republicans' brilliant electoral strategy is to keep the Democrats from getting 800,000 more votes nationwide in the 2028, but in process do everything in their power to alienate the 800,000 Latinos who get the right to vote this year and every year between now and the 2028 election.

And it is not just the Latino tsunami Republicans are facing. Americans by a wide majority, typically in upper 60 percent, favor some kind of a pathway to citizenship. At those levels the independent voters have clearly weighed in.

The Republicans may have a respectable showing in the 2014 election. Off-year elections in a president's second term are tough for his party. But beyond 2014 the prospects for Republicans on a national level are grim. If Republicans continue to block immigration reform, I cannot for the life of me see how they survive as a national party.

February 5, 2014

Self-Defeating Politics

I have a friend who is a very successful banker at one of the large national banks. We have never discussed what he makes, but I am sure it is well into six figures. As one might expect from a successful banker, he is a rather conservative fellow.

He and I were recently discussing politics. He told me that he had voted a straight Republican ticket his entire life but that he would never again vote for any Republican. I asked why and he told me because "they have insulted my family and disrespected my father."

You see, my friend's father came to the United States illegally from Mexico in the 1950s specifically so that his children would have a chance at the life my friend is living today. His father eventually became a citizen as result of Ronald Reagan's immigration reform in 1986. Reagan was a hero to his family for championing their cause. Now Republicans are calling his father a criminal.

I do not know what Republican strategist came up with the idea of making immigration a wedge issue, but one almost has to wonder if it was not a Democratic saboteur. Take the fastest growing demographic group in the country, and one that is inclined to agree with your party on a wide variety of cultural issues, and then do everything you can to alienate it. Brilliant.

This is one political calculus the George W. Bush-Karl Rove team had right. While governor, Bush reached out to Latinos and liberally appointed them to a wide variety of commissions and benches. As president, he pushed hard for comprehensive immigration reform.

As a result he consistently won about 40 percent to 45 percent of the Latino vote, seriously cutting into what had been considered part of the Democratic base.

But after months of anti-immigrant vitriol in the Republican primaries in 2008, John McCain's share of the Latino vote dropped to the low 30s, notwithstanding his relatively moderate stance on immigration. Considering Barak Obama's margin of victory in 2008, it can hardly be argued that the immigration issue was a deciding factor in the election. But looking forward to 2012 and even more to 2016, a growing Latino population (and its growing voting participation) could easily be a deciding factor, especially in the swing states of Florida, Colorado, and New Mexico.

Political parties attempting to tap into anti-immigrant fervor is not new. Throughout our country's history, various parties have tried to exploit the anxiety that normally accompanies large waves of immigration. Parties like the American Party (1850s), the Immigration Restriction League (1890s), and my person favorite, the aptly named, Know Nothing Party (1850s), are a few of those. Chances are you have never heard of any of these, which, of course, speaks volumes on the long-term viability of such a strategy.

Almost all of the Republican strategists and elected officials with whom I visit understand that, regardless how they view the policy issues, the immigration issue is an unfolding political disaster for their party. Increasingly Republican activists are attempting to take back the issue by promoting reasonable immigration reform and tone down the anti-Latino rhetoric. For example, earlier this year in Texas a watered-down version of Arizona's immigration legislation was defeated notwithstanding large Republican majorities in both houses of the legislature. Among the leading opponents were conservative Republican business executives.

I realized the degree to which the rhetoric had changed recently while watching a segment on immigration on Fox News. Normally, the "pro-immigration" talking head would have been some far left Democratic Latino member of Congress. Instead, there were two attractive, young female Republican strategists making the case *for* immigration reform. The talking head making the case against reform was some old windbag who could barely string two sentences together. This reframing of the issue on the most conservative news network hardly seemed accidental.

Behind closed doors, Republicans and Democrats in Congress have agreed on the basics of immigration reform. Improve border security. Have guest worker program and allow immigrants to come and go. Tamper-proof ID. A procedure that allows immigrants who came here illegally, or were brought here illegally as children, to gain a legal status after satisfying certain conditions. There are some details to be worked out, but it is not rocket science, and polls show that a large majority of Americans favor this type of moderate, common-sense approach.

But both political parties, for different reasons, have incentives not to solve the problem. Republicans, after having let the genie out of the bottle, now are petrified of the issue in their own primaries. In the meantime, as long as there is no solution, Democrats can continue to paint Republicans as the anti-Latino party. What began as a Republican wedge issue has ironically become a wedge issue for Democrats to peel Latino voters away from the Republican Party.

This quagmire is yet another example of how our two-party, hyper-partisan system is broken. Of all of the problems we face today, and they are certainly numerous and daunting, getting our immigration system fixed is one of the easiest to address. And yet because of the bitter, toxic political milieu in which we find ourselves, our immigration policy is adrift with no land in sight.

September 7, 2011

Gift That Keeps on Giving

ccording to one press account, attendees at a House Minority Leader Nancy Pelosi dinner party broke out in spontaneous celebration at the news of House Majority Leader Eric Cantor's defeat in the Virginia Republican primary by a relatively unknown challenger last week. Given the depth of the partisan animosity in Washington, the reaction may have been pure *schadenfreude*. But I suspect it may have also been because the Democrats gathered at Pelosi's party realized that Cantor's loss probably means there will be no comprehensive immigration reform for some time.

Now you are probably saying, "What are you talking about? Democrats are in favor of immigration reform." And you are right. They are. But the truth is, the current logjam over immigration reform in Washington is a political gift to Democrats that just keeps on giving.

Every year that rolls by without solving the immigration problem, another 800,000 Latinos who are U.S. citizens turn 18 and become eligible to vote. Many of those coming of age are deeply resentful of Republicans, who they believe have disparaged and disrespected their family members by calling them criminals. They also hold Republicans responsible for keeping their older brothers and sisters and friends, who were brought here as children, in a legal purgatory with no way out.

And as the immigration issue continues to fester, Republicans are beginning to alienate other groups traditionally sympathetic to their ideas. Recently, a coalition of Latino evangelicals has been joined by other evangelicals in demanding immigration reform. Republicans do not seem to understand that because someone agrees with you on abortion does not mean they will vote for you so you can deport their grandmother. Of course, the business community, a traditional Republican funding source, has long since split the sheets with the Republican grass roots on this issue.

And then there is the matter of that vast majority of Americans who want to see immigration reform that includes a legal status for those who came here illegally. A poll released just this week by the Public Religion Research Institute and the Brookings Institution found that 79 percent of Americans favor some kind of legal status for unlawful immigrants. A pathway to full citizenship is favored by 62 percent of Americans. Only 19 percent now say that those who came here without a visa should be deported. How you can expect to win national elections when you take positions that 80 percent of the American people oppose is a mystery to me and many others.

The problem for the Republican Party is that the 19 percent who want to deport everyone dominate their grass roots and primaries. Ironically, the polls show that even a majority of Republicans favor immigration reform that includes a pathway to citizenship. But the turnout in primaries is so low that they tend to be dominated by those with the most extreme views. Which is why we need to reform the primary system, but I digress.

Almost every Republican candidate who came through the editorial board this year told us that immigration was the hot button issue for Republican primary voters. So to get through a Republican primary, candidates have to take a position on immigration that is at odds with a sweeping majority of Americans and increasingly political suicide by demography for the party.

Ironically, Cantor's loss may not have really been all that

attributable to the immigration issue. Erick Erickson, a well-known conservative blogger and columnist, has a piece on FoxNews.com arguing that Cantor's loss had more to do with his personal style and political ineptness than it did about immigration. It is always risky to read too much into the results of local elections regarding national issues. As former U.S. House Speaker Tip O'Neill famously quipped, "All politics is local."

But in politics, perception is often reality. And there is no doubt that Cantor's loss has thrown up a serious road block to what was increasingly looking like a move toward a compromise on immigration this year. And if nothing is done before the 2014 election, it is even harder to imagine getting anything done in the lead-up to a presidential election.

And it will be an unmitigated disaster for Republicans if they go into 2016 with immigration reform still on the table. You simply cannot lose 70 percent to 80 percent of the Latino vote and put together an Electoral College majority. So there may well have been a bottle of champagne popped at the Clinton home as well last week when the results from Virginia came in.

June 15, 2014

Broken Brains Are to Blame

Once again, we are faced with a mindless murderous rampage in which innocent people going about their daily lives were gunned down by a complete stranger.

Once again, after an exhaustive investigation the murderer's motive will be incomprehensible to normal people.

Once again, the pro-gun and anti-gun forces will shout their arguments, the ones we have all heard countless times already, but at even higher decibel levels.

Once again, we will bury the dead and try to memorialize the lives senselessly cut short. Once again, we will become slightly more numb to this kind of incident. And once again, we will do nothing to prevent the next tragedy.

Even after the Washington Navy Yard shooting, the pattern will be repeated, not addressing the real issue: broken brain chemistry.

First, of course, this will be more fodder for the gun debate. I am a gun owner who shoots frequently and believes the Second Amendment was intended by the framers to protect the right of the individual to protect himself or herself from both criminal and tyrannical government. But I also recognize that no right is unlimited.

We do not allow individuals to "bear arms" by owning their own tanks or rocket-propelled grenade launchers. And it would not bother me to further restrict assault rifles and magazine sizes and have universal background checks on the off chance such restrictions might prevent one of these disasters.

But at the same, it seems clear that further restrictions such as these almost certainly will not stop future mass shootings. They certainly would not have stopped the Navy Yard rampage, as the shooter used a Remington 870 pump shotgun and passed a background check.

For those of you not familiar with guns, a Remington 870 is a very popular shotgun frequently used for hunting. According to Remington, more than 10 million had been manufactured. For generations, it has been given to many youngsters, including me, as their first shotgun because of the simplicity of its operation and safety record.

Not even the most ardent gun control advocates have ever suggested that guns like the 870 should be banned, and it is even available in countries that highly regulate firearms, like Britain.

And there will be a variety of other arguments trotted out again. I have already heard a debate between commentators about the role of video games.

With incidents such as the Navy Yard shooting, we continue to try to deal with this problem as though we were dealing with rational actors, which we most assuredly are not. The simple fact is that a person commits this kind of unthinkable act because his or her thinking is horrifically broken. This problem at its core is a fundamental breakdown in the person's brain chemistry. And until we understand how a person's brain chemistry goes this awry and how to prevent it, we are going to continue to bury the dead.

President Barack Obama's recent proposal to spend $100 million on brain research is a step in the right direction, although $100 million seems a paltry amount. Decoding the human genome cost nearly $4 billion, and Europe and China both have brain research initiatives up and running and have already spent much more. Hopefully, his proposal will not get balled up with the current Washington dysfunction and opposed by Republicans just because the president proposed it.

But an even more aggressive moon-shot type initiative on brain research could yield many benefits. Serious mental illness is still the leading cause of homelessness. It might also give us some insights and even possible solutions for problems like substance abuse and other brain disorders such as Alzheimer's.

And at the end of the day, such an initiative, regardless of the costs, could potentially save billions. According to the Alzheimer's Organization, that disease alone currently costs us more than $200 billion annually, of which nearly 75 percent is paid by Medicare or Medicaid. And that cost is projected to rise rapidly as our population ages.

So spending a few billion trying to get our hands around what goes on in the brain, and more important, what goes wrong in the brain, would likely be money well-spent. And it might, just might, lead to a day when no one gets a call that a loved one has been senselessly gunned down by a madman.

September 21, 2013

The Madness Continues

O nce again we are faced with mayhem, caused by a single individual with a weapon that is easily obtainable. Once again, family members mourn the loss of an innocent father, brother and son. Once again, the family and friends of the shooter are devastated and bewildered. And once again we attempt to understand the shooting in rational terms. Was he a member of an anti-government cult? Did he have a grudge against Transportation Security Administration workers?

No. There is no rational explanation for this type of behavior because it is irrational. It is the result not of some ideology but of a broken brain. The sooner we accept this obvious conclusion, the sooner we might find a solution for these incidents.

David Eagleman is a neuroscientist at Baylor College of Medicine. In his book *Incognito* he describes the case of a man with normal sexual behavior until he reached his mid-40s. His wife noticed that he began to develop an interest in child pornography, which ultimately became an obsession. At the same time, he began to have headaches.

His wife persuaded the man to go to the doctor, and after a series of tests, a brain tumor was discovered. After the tumor was removed, his behavior returned to normal.

A few months after the surgery, the man began to have pedophiliac thoughts again. He went back to the doctors, and they determined that the surgery had missed a piece of the tumor and that it had begun to grow back. A second surgery completely removed the tumor, and the man never suffered from pedophilia again.

Most of us who grew up in Texas also remember the case of Charles Whitman, the sniper atop the University of Texas at Austin tower who in 1966 killed 13 people and wounded 30 more. Whitman left a suicide note in which he said he had begun to have strange, uncontrollable thoughts of violence and asked that his brain be examined after his death to prevent future tragedies. An autopsy revealed a brain tumor.

Our entire existential experience is based on our belief that we are in control of our mind and that the picture it paints of the world around us is accurate.

To doubt this fundamental premise frightens us to the core because to do so means that some physical abnormality in our brain could cause us not to be in control of what we do, even to the extent of doing one of these terrible things ourselves.

We base our social interactions, including our justice system, on the belief that everyone has free will.

All we need to do, the conventional wisdom goes, is set up the proper incentives and disincentives for the behaviors we want to encourage and discourage.

For the vast majority of human beings—whose brains are working correctly—it is a formula that works. But for those whose free will has been hijacked by aberrant brain mechanics, it is a meaningless dynamic.

One of the reasons we are loath to start down the road of questioning our fundamental beliefs regarding culpability is that there is no clear place to stop.

Cases like Eagleman's patient or Whitman, where a tumor is physically impinging on a portion of the brain, may be clear. But what if a person just has a low serotonin level and, thus, is prone to certain mental illnesses? Should that affect their culpability for their actions?

At what point do brain mechanics become every criminal's excuse?

The truth is that we are just beginning to understand how the brain functions and how to treat abnormalities. It was only a few decades ago that we were chopping out huge portions of the brain in lobotomies. There should be few priorities higher than getting this figured out. The costs of not doing so are unbearable.

The incident last week at LAX will inevitably mean even tighter security at airports, which will cost billions and make air travel even more inconvenient than it is now—if that is possible.

The costs of broken brains ripple through our society in countless other ways, from overwhelmed emergency rooms to jail overcrowding to gun violence to homelessness. The list is endless.

We need to act, and act now. We need to spend whatever it takes. If we do not, the list of victims will continue to grow and the costs will continue to mount.

November 6, 2013

Let's Invest in Mental Health

Oddly, as we have come to better understand mental illness over the last several decades, there has been a corresponding reduction in our investment to deal with it.

Nationally between 1955 and 2005 the number of psychiatric hospital beds plummeted from 558,000 to just 53,000, according to the Treatment Advocacy Center, a nonprofit that studies mental illness.

The U.S. population, meanwhile, grew dramatically during that time, reducing the number of beds available per capita from 340 per 100,000 individuals down to 17. Recently, another study found that the number of beds per capita in 2010 had fallen again to about 14.

As bad as the national situation is, in our region it is even worse. After a psychiatric hospital closed last year due to a lack of funds, local mental health officials estimated that we are now down to just two beds per 100,000 people.

According to the National Institute of Mental Health, schizophrenia alone affects about 1 percent of the population.

With more than 6 million people in our region, that means we probably have about 60,000 of our neighbors who suffer from schizophrenia. That is about one bed for every 500 individuals with schizophrenia in our region.

I do not mean to suggest that every schizophrenic needs to be hospitalized, but many need a permanent place to live where they can be supervised, and many more need episodic hospitalization.

Add to that group those suffering from severe depression, bipolar disorder, Alzheimer's and a host of other mental illnesses and it is readily apparent that our facilities are woefully inadequate to deal with the mentally ill in our community.

Instead of providing treatment, we leave thousands of the mentally ill on the street to fend for themselves or jail them when they become too much of a nuisance or too threatening. Thousands more are a crushing burden on families that struggle to care for them. For a community that prides itself on its faith-based values, this is an unconscionable situation.

Every great faith tradition teaches we have a duty to care for those who are vulnerable. Jesus specifically mentioned how we care for the sick and afflicted as one of the criteria by which our lives will be judged.

I recently sat down with state Sen. John Whitmire, a Houston Democrat who has long studied the effect of mental illness on our criminal justice system. Whitmire told me that when he is lobbying his colleagues for more funding for mental health initiatives, he frequently chides them that "if you won't do it for the right reasons, then do it because it will save us money." He is so right.

The cost of not addressing the needs of our fellow citizens struggling with a mental illness is incalculable.

The never-ending mass shooting incidents that dominate cable news coverage are but the most dramatic of these consequences.

When you tally the incidental costs of the homeless, petty crime, our jail bulging with mentally ill inmates, health care costs at our public hospitals and thousands of police calls for mental illness-related incidents, we could save many millions of dollars by making an intelligent investment in mental health facilities and care.

I will not presume to suggest what form such an investment should take. That decision should be based on a community discussion led by our elected officials and mental health care providers. But it is clear that this is not a one-size-fits-all problem.

Mental illness is as complex and nuanced as the brain itself. We will need to pursue many different strategies based on individuals' particular illness, family situation and many other factors.

Going out and building some grand new mental health hospital may be needed, but it alone will not be sufficient. And we will need the state's help. For far too long our state officials have been penny-wise and pound-foolish on this issue.

We need to prepare our legislative agenda this year and be ready to go to Austin in the 2015 session and make the case that an additional investment in mental health is both the right thing and the smart thing to do.

January 29, 2014

Basics of Drug Policy Reform

The premise that underpins our criminal justice system is that people have the free will to choose between right and wrong, at least as right and wrong are defined by law. We impose a penalty on those who have, of their own free will, made the wrong decision. We do this in the belief that the punishment will deter them from making the same choice in the future and will deter others from making similar bad choices.

When we determine that people did not act of their own free will, such as when a person is legally insane, we excuse that person from the consequences of his or her actions.

The idea that the sale and use of drugs should be illegal largely arose in the first half of the 20th century, when we had little understanding of the science of addiction. Then, and even now to a large degree, the abuse of drugs is seen as a moral failing—a bad exercise of free will. However, science is increasingly showing that the use of drugs actually changes our brain chemistry and thus affects our ability to make the very moral judgments implicit in the criminal justice paradigm. The National Institutes of Health defines drug addiction as "a chronic, relapsing brain disease that is characterized by compulsive drug seeking and use, despite harmful consequences." The NIH goes on to say, "It is considered a brain disease because drugs change the brain—they change its structure and how it works."

The NIH concludes that while the initial decision to use drugs is mostly voluntary, once a person becomes addicted, it is not. If that is true and we are punishing people who are not acting out of free will, the entire logical underpinning of our criminal justice system is called into question.

In addition to basing the criminalization of drug use on a questionable theoretical legal basis, the many practical negative effects of criminalization have been well documented.

Accidental poisonings from drug overdoses now lead automobile accidents as the leading cause of accidental death in the country. Virtually all of these overdose deaths are attributable to addicts receiving adulterated drugs or doses of varying purity and strength. Even the most dangerous and addictive drugs, when administered in medically controlled conditions, rarely result in the death of the patient.

To mark the 40th anniversary of the War on Drugs last year, *Time* magazine published a list of the 10 worst side-effects of the war (http://healthland.time.com/2011/06/17/top-10-unhealthy-side-effects-of-the-war-on-drugs/#richard-m-nixon). It is a sobering list.

Among these is the fact that an increasingly large share of HIV infections are due to addicts sharing tainted needles. One study estimated that through 2009 contaminated needles had caused 290,000 HIV infections. One study in Europe found that 60 percent of all new HIV infections were caused by drug injections rather that sex.

The economic costs of the attempt to interdict drugs and incarcerate users runs in the hundreds of billions of dollars. The U.S. incarceration rate at the start of the War on Drugs was just over 100 per 100,000 Americans. Today it is more than 700 per 100,000.

August Vollmer was a police chief in the first half of the 20th century in California. He was a trailblazer in modern law enforcement techniques and served as president of the International Association of Police Chiefs in 1921. He is frequently referred to as the Father of Modern Law Enforcement. The push to criminalize drug use largely arose during his career. In a 1936 paper on the subject, Vollmer said,

"Drug addiction ... is not a police problem; it never has been, and never can be solved by policemen. It is first and last a medical problem." It makes one wonder where we would be today if his advice had been heeded.

A few years ago, Bruce Willis starred in the movie *Siege*. In the movie, Willis plays an Army general. There have been a series of terrorist attacks in New York, and the president is considering sending in the Army to track down those responsible. Willis is asked his opinion about using the Army for this purpose. In arguing against the deployment, he answered, "The Army is a broadsword, not a scalpel." Increasingly, it appears that we have mistakenly been using weapons of war in our attempts to deal with our drug problem instead of medical instruments.

With the exception of a few people who make a living from the War on Drugs, virtually no one thinks those weapons are working. Polling consistently shows that about 70 percent of Americans agree. It seems that it is only a matter of time before we try a different approach.

A detailed plan is far beyond the scope of this column or my expertise. However, if we are to have a more effective drug policy, there would appear to be a few fundamental principles upon which it should be based.

The goal of the policy should be to reduce drug abuse and addiction. Make no mistake, drug abuse and addiction (including alcohol and tobacco abuse) are a bane of mankind. If we could wave a magic wand and make every recreational drug disappear, we would all be better off. But recreational drug use goes back as far as we have recorded history. It is not going to magically disappear. However, we should never allow that inevitability to lead us to conclude we should just throw up our hands and give in to unrestricted drug use and distribution. First and foremost our policy should be focused on mitigating the monstrous cost that abuse and addiction inflict on our species.

Children must be prevented from starting drug use. The research clearly shows that most addiction begins at a young age, when our brains are still developing critical decision-making skills. Young people, for the most part, simply are not prepared to weigh the risks of the potentially life-altering decision about whether to use drugs. And again by drugs, I am including alcohol and tobacco. While it appears that the criminal enforcement of drug laws has been largely ineffective and in some ways counterproductive, the one exception I would make is for any adult providing drugs to an adolescent. Anyone who does should be subject to swift, sure and severe punishment.

All drugs are not the same. Different drugs have very different effects on us. Therefore, we need a nuanced policy that reflects these differences. As a general proposition, we should impose greater restrictions on the more dangerous drugs. As simple as that proposition may sound, our current policy is far from it. For example, tobacco and alcohol are responsible for 20 times more deaths than all illegal drugs combined. Yet we impose minimal restrictions on tobacco and alcohol.

The most glaring example of this disparity, however, is the treatment of marijuana. Some estimate that 80 percent of the War on Drugs is devoted to stopping marijuana trafficking. But the deleterious effects of marijuana pale by comparison to tobacco or alcohol. There has yet to be a single recorded death from an overdose of marijuana. Marijuana is also much less frequently involved in incidental criminal behavior than alcohol because it induces passivity in the user, while alcohol reduces inhibition and encourages risky behaviors.

The hypocrisy implicit when we base our drug policies on societal biases rather than an objective scientific assessment of the risks undermines the moral authority of society to regulate drug use at all.

Invest in research. If we ever arrive at a final solution to the drug problem, it will come from medical breakthroughs on how we treat addiction. Already, there are medicines that block the effects of alcohol and cocaine, but they must be taken daily, which an addict is unlikely to do. There has also been some promising research on drug vaccines that permanently negate the effect of drugs. A cocaine vaccine has been tested on mice with promising results.

Whether it is the development of vaccines that prevent addiction or some other discovery about brain chemistry and addiction, this type of medical research is the most promising hope for a real, permanent solution. Given the enormous cost of drug abuse and addiction, almost any investment one can imagine in research in this area could be justified on a cost-benefits analysis.

In this country, politicians rarely even question the war on drugs for fear their opponents will accuse them of being soft on drugs, notwithstanding that 70 percent of the American people have figured out that what we are doing is not working. Unfortunately, as in so many cases, most of our elected officials continue to lead from the rear.

April 11 and April 25, 2012

How We Think About Homelessness

It was a crisp but bitterly cold night. Park Avenue's holiday decorations and Christmas carols intermittently carried on as a north wind created a festive mood in those walking along with me. I was headed to one of New York City's landmark hotel bars for drinks with friends.

I almost walked by her without even noticing her, huddled beneath a blanket on an exhaust grate attempting to capture its heat. She was mumbling incomprehensibly, almost certainly the product of a schizophrenia-infested mind.

Something in her voice drew my eyes to her face, and I went cold. She was older, probably 70s, although it is hard to judge the age of someone who lives on the street. What stopped me dead in my tracks was the fact that her face bore a remarkable resemblance to my mother's, so much so that I stumbled doing a double-take.

I stood there stunned for several minutes, frantic that I had to do something. But what? Would she even accept any help? And what could I do to help her? Give her cash? That undoubtedly would be stolen from her within minutes. Check her into a hotel? They probably would not accept her. Go get a police officer? He was standing a little more than a block away already.

Ultimately I did what most of us do when we are confronted with the mentally ill in public spaces ... I did nothing. Instead, I walked away to meet my friends in a nice warm bar.

But I could not, I cannot, get her pitiful, helpless face out of my mind. I am overwhelmed by guilt that we, that I, allow about a half-million of our fellow Americans to sleep on the street every night. How is it that the richest country in the history of world can leave hundreds of thousands on the street every night, including the sick and elderly? How is it that a country that loudly and frequently proclaims its Judeo-Christian values can allow such suffering to continue in plain sight?

It begins with a misconception. Most people think that homelessness is an economic issue or a substance abuse issue. But in reality it is mostly a mental illness issue. Most homelessness experts estimate that 70 percent to 80 percent of the homeless have a moderate to severe mental illness.

That is not something most of us want to accept. If a person is living on the street because they will not work or because they do alcohol or drugs, that allows us to assuage our conscience that they have, at least in part, brought this on themselves. The fact that most are there because their brain chemistry is not functioning properly is an uncomfortable proposition because it makes our indifference all the more contemptible.

It is also a discouraging fact because there are no real "cures" for most serious mental illnesses. The best case in most instances is to manage the mental illness with prescription drugs.

Yet we have this myth in our collective public mind that all we need to do is get these people back on their feet and into a job and everything will be fine. It is myth that is perpetuated to some degree by the homeless agencies. They love to trot out their success stories of someone who was just down on his or her luck and has now, with the help of the homeless agency of course, turned life around.

The truth is that those success stories are the exception. Unfortunately, most of the mentally ill homeless will never get any better without some kind of intervention. Most of the homeless will need our help for the rest of their lives.

Recently, a veteran of one of Houston's marquee homelessness agencies told me that 70 percent to 80 percent of the homeless will need one or more social services forever. That tale is not nearly as inspiring and, consequentially, not one likely to motivate people to give money to homeless agencies. But it is the reality. And it is one with which we must come to grips.

June 8, 2013

Homelessness and Mental Illness

I recently toured a large homeless facility. The manifestation of mental illnesses was everywhere. As I moved through the facility speaking to its residents, I could not help but wonder where their families were. Why was there not a son or a daughter or a parent taking care of these lost souls?

The reality is that the burden on families of a severely mentally ill family member is severe. Many if not most families will valiantly try to provide personal care for their loved one. Government resources are scarce, leaving families with few affordable alternatives. You would have to find private care, which is astronomically expensive, or do what many families are forced to do: simply give up and let their loved ones roam the streets.

Homelessness is a complex, nuanced problem. There is not one solution or strategy that fits all cases of homelessness. But that does not mean it is insoluble.

But let's be clear: This is not a resource problem. There have been some estimates that simply housing all of the homeless in our country would cost about $20 billion annually, which is about what we spend every two months on the Afghan war. And that amount most likely could easily be recovered in costs we now incur because we are not addressing the problem.

Another way to think about the scale of the problem is this: There are something like 350,000 churches, synagogues and mosques in this country. Every one of these represents a faith tradition that teaches we have a responsibility to care for the sick and the poor. We could provide the necessary care if each one of these houses of worship accepted responsibility for only one person with a mental illness.

The larger problem is how we think about mental illness generally. The care we provide for those who suffer from chronic mental illness stands in stark contrast to the care we provide those who are physically ill. No one would even consider leaving a person who had been physically injured on the side of the road and not call for help. Yet we walk by the mentally ill languishing on the street without so much as a second glance. And when our friends come down with even mildest of seasonal viruses, we all rush to provide chicken soup and other remedies. Yet we rarely offer help to families who are struggling to care for a loved one stricken with mental illness.

We feel and react differently to mental illness. It makes us uncomfortable, in part because we do not understand it. So much of who we are as human beings relies on the dependable interaction with others, and when that dependability is disrupted, it is very disconcerting.

We also still cling to notions that mental illness is somehow self-inflicted or the result of moral weakness or substance abuse. But science is teaching us that most mental illness is the result of brain chemistry gone awry, really not that much different from any other system in our body breaking down. We are also beginning to learn that much of the substance abuse in our society is the result of mental illness, not the other way around.

There are certainly homeless individuals who do not suffer from a mental illness. People lose their jobs and don't have any savings. Sometimes individuals or families come here looking for work without sufficient savings to make the transition. Women and children often end up homeless as the result of domestic violence. But these cases are a minority, and they are cases in which homeless agencies can more readily provide help that will get them back on their feet.

And I do not in any way mean to diminish the work done to help the homeless who do not suffer from a mental illness. We certainly need to maintain a safety net for those individuals who temporarily find themselves in the lurch. But we will never make a serious dent in the homeless issue unless and until we come to grips with how to deal with the homeless population that suffers from mental illness.

June 12, 2013

Homelessness: Changing the Law

L ast week I suggested that mental illness plays a larger role in
the homelessness issue than we realize, or perhaps are willing
to admit. In 1955 there were more than 500,000 hospital beds
in the United States available to treat mental illness. Today there are
only about 60,000.

I think all of us will agree there has not been a commensurate decline in the number of individuals with a mental illness. To the contrary, psychiatric studies show that serious mental illness consistently
affects about 6 percent of the population. And our population has
about doubled since 1955. Rather, this decline in institutional care is
a stunning abdication of our responsibility to provide care for some
of the most vulnerable among us.

There are many reasons for this sorry state of affairs. Most promi-
nently, beginning in the 1960s our legal system made a dramatic shift
in its approach to the institutionalization of individuals who have
a mental illness. Confining someone to mental hospital came to be
judged under the same constitutional standards as a person being
incarcerated for a crime. At the time, it was heralded as another wave
of the civil rights awakening sweeping the country. As a result, thousands with serious mental illnesses were simply discharged, and we,
as a society, decided that we would no longer "force" care on those
with a mental illness.

Predictably, most people with a mental illness do not seek the
treatment they need. With the advances in drug therapies over the last

two decades, many could lead relatively normal and productive lives if they stayed on their medications. But if they are living unsupervised on the street, the likelihood of that happening is almost nil. Frequently, these individuals will self-medicate with other drugs, most often alcohol. In retrospect, one cannot help wonder if "forcing" care on people with mental illness should really be judged by the same standards we use to deprive criminals of their liberty. I do not believe that when the framers crafted the Bill of Rights they intended to include a guaranteed right to freeze to death on a sidewalk because your defective brain chemistry is not telling you to come in out of the cold.

This "enlightened" view of the medical care for those with mental illness meant that financially strapped state and local governments could save millions by cutting back on building and operating mental hospitals. Concern over the civil rights of the mental ill became a convenient excuse to not fund mental health facilities and programs.

Ironically, the savings have been largely illusory. Instead, individuals with chronic mental illness have exploded our jail populations and wreaked all kinds of havoc in society at large, from mass shootings to routine domestic violence. It is truly a case of being penny-wise and pound-foolish.

Dr. Ken Mattox, the longtime director of Ben Taub General Hospital, told me that approximately 30 percent of the hospital's emergency admissions involve people with a mental illness who have injured themselves or someone else, typically their caregiver.

The starting point for any discussion of how we end homelessness must be a re-examination of how we treat mental illness, and, in particular, our legal procedures for "forcing" care on individuals with mental illness. Making it too easy to commit individuals is a slippery slope and subject to abuse. But our legal system makes all kinds of nuanced judgments in other areas. There is no reason we cannot do so in this area as well.

Some states have begun experimenting with commitment procedures based on treatment failures. For example, if individuals fail to stay on their medications after a certain number of attempts, they can be committed to a treatment facility where caregivers can be certain that the proper dosages of medications are taken. And given the substantial improvement in drug therapies for the common mental illness in the last couple of decades, this could make a real difference.

We will have to feel our way along in sorting out how and when care is forced on someone. But simply punting and pretending that these individuals can be responsible for their own care, which pretty much is our current strategy, is not acceptable.

June 15, 2013

Homelessness: A Worthy Legacy

L ast night in Houston about 7,000 to 8,000 men, women and children were homeless. About half of those found temporary shelter with one of our local homelessness service agencies. The rest slept on the street. Experts estimate that 50 percent to 80 percent of these individuals have a moderate or serious mental illness, depending how you count and what definitions you use.

The sad truth is that once a mentally ill person becomes homeless, he or she is likely to die that way. If our delivery systems of mental health services continue to get shorted on resources as they have, that is the fate many of those 7,000 to 8,000 people face, as will thousands more who will follow them.

Over the last half century our country has become increasingly apathetic about individuals with chronic mental illness, and especially those who become homeless. It has become just one more of those insurmountable social problems that no one seems to have the time or resources to address.

But recently something has changed. Tragedies like the mass shootings in Aurora, Colo., and at Sandy Hook Elementary School in Connecticut have focused public opinion on the collateral damage that can be inflicted when mental illness goes untreated. Increasingly, government and nongovernment organizations are stepping up efforts to deal with chronic mental illness.

In our own city, Mayor Annise Parker's administration has recently announced a new program that will prioritize housing for the most vulnerable homeless populations. This "housing-first" strategy represents the emerging theory that, to have any chance to stabilize these individuals, we must first get them off the street. While just providing housing will not solve the problem, it is unquestionably true that nothing constructive or positive happens in these folks' lives while they are living on the street.

We may be at a tipping point. The public seems increasingly prepared to provide the resources to address this problem. In part, because it is the humane and compassionate thing to do, but also because we are increasingly becoming aware that it is in our own enlightened self-interest to do so.

At the same time, our understanding of mental illness is rapidly advancing. Today, more than any time in the past, drugs are available that can make a real difference in the lives of people struggling with mental illness. If we can provide a mechanism to make sure the individuals who need them get and take the proper dosages, it would be a vast improvement over the current situation. As long as we engage in the fantasy that people whose brain chemistry is flawed can and will make rational decisions about their treatment, we will continue to have thousands living on the street.

I began this series by describing an encounter I had with a homeless woman in New York a few months ago who bore an uncanny resemblance to my own mother. The moment yielded an epiphany. Since that night on Park Avenue, I have thought about what I would have done had the woman I saw shivering under a blanket actually been my mother. I would have done the same thing you would have done if it had been your mother. Any of us would have scooped her up in our arms and taken her to a warm, safe place even if her mental illness may have caused her to resist our help.

If we would do that for our own mother, how can we justify doing anything less for someone else's mother or father, son or daughter?

It seems only fitting that Houston should lead the country in solving this problem once and for all. This is the city that can put a man on the moon, where medical miracles like intricate heart surgery flourish and where technological innovations can lead explorers to hit a spot the size of a grapefruit two miles under the Gulf of Mexico with a drill bit. Finding the resources and legal mechanisms to provide humane, constructive care for a few thousand people that we have heretofore abandoned to the street hardly seems a daunting task by comparison.

What a wonderful legacy this city and this generation could leave if we were to show the rest of the country and the world that our fellow Houstonians with chronic mentally illness do not have to live—and die—on the street.

June 22, 2013

Hurricane Preparedness
(And Lack Thereof)

L ast week, to mark the beginning of hurricane season, *Houston Chronicle* science reporter Eric Berger wrote an article reporting how little has been done to reduce the area's vulnerability to a major hurricane since Ike. Also, Phil Bedient and James Blackburn, of Rice's SSPEED Center, a severe storm think tank, made the case in an editorial for greater efforts to reduce the area's vulnerability to hurricanes.

There has been a great deal of negative or skeptical reaction to their calls for action. This reaction has mostly fallen into two categories.

First, there are those who do not live close to the shore and who argue that the cost of such projects is not justified to protect primarily beach homes, which they argue should never have been built in such vulnerable areas in the first place. And if that was the objective of hurricane mitigation projects, I would agree.

But while such sentiments have a certain popular appeal, they miss the point that hurricane mitigation efforts have little to do with beach homes. Actually, not much can be done to protect homes directly on the beach. In fact, all of the surge protection concepts that have surfaced to date, like Bill Merrill's "Ike Dike," would be constructed behind beachfront homes, providing them no protection.

But hurricanes do not stop at the beach. The effects of a major storm will be felt over a wide area in many ways.

First, the hurricane surge area is huge. Because we live on a flat coastal plain with an elongated continental shelf, we are particularly vulnerable to storm surges that can extend many miles inland. For a Category 5 storm, the projected surge area covers nearly all of Galveston County, about 60 percent of Brazoria County and 20 percent of Harris County. In this area are the homes of almost 1 million people, along with thousands of schools, churches and hospitals.

There are also major employment centers like the Houston Ship Channel and the plants along its banks, University of Texas Medical Branch at Galveston, NASA's Johnson Space Center, and the Ports of Galveston and Texas City. It includes refineries that produce a large percentage of the country's gasoline and jet fuel. A major storm that flooded this entire area would have devastating economic repercussions. Gas prices would soar. Tens of thousands would be out of work for months affecting every business in the region.

There are also very troubling potential environmental impacts. This region is chock full of hazardous waste sites, including several superfund sites. At least one of these, in the Texas City area, is surrounded by only a 14-foot levee. A storm surge that overtops a number of these waste sites and spreads their materials over hundreds of square miles could have long-term, devastating effects on the entire region.

If you live in west Harris County and think a major hurricane will not affect your life, trust me you are wrong.

There were also those who expressed a fatalistic viewpoint, basically arguing that you cannot fight nature. But we know that is not true. The Dutch have been doing it successfully for hundreds of years. Also, coastal cities all around the globe are proactively dealing with the threat of storm flooding. The fact that Houston is one of the few vulnerable cities in the world that is not doing anything to protect itself is anathema to our civic heritage.

There is, however, considerable room for reasonable disagreement about what we should do. Scientists at Texas A&M at Galveston and Rice as well as others have been studying the issue. Many alternatives, both structural and non-structural, have been discussed.

Also we should recognize that storm surge mitigation efforts should not be the sole focus. The studies that looked at the economic impact of Ike suggest that the fact much of the city had no electricity for weeks may have taken the largest economic toll. So hardening the electrical grid must be on the table. There are also issues around upland flooding of bayous that could occur many miles from where storm surges stops.

How we approach this issue will probably be the most important decision our region will make in this century. We certainly should take our time and be deliberate in the process and make sure we get this right. Any investment must be judged by a rigorous cost-benefit analysis, and as a matter of equity those who benefit the most from any improvements should pay the largest share of the costs.

But the problem is complacency. And every year that passes without a major storm event will tend to increase our complacency.

In the first half of the 20th century the Dutch, distracted by two world wars, let down their defenses against the North Sea. As a result, in 1953 a major storm flooded nearly 500 square miles and killed almost 2,000 people. It was then that the Dutch reinvigorated their commitment to protect their country from the North Sea.

Had Ike made landfall 30-40 miles farther down the Texas coast, the resulting disaster would have made the 1953 Dutch storm look tame by comparison. There would have been many more casualties and a much larger area flooded. I pray that we will not have to suffer such a tragedy to shake us out of our lethargy.

June 8, 2011

Sensible Approach to Climate Change

According to NASA, global temperatures have been rising since about 1880. The space agency also tells us that 20 of the warmest years on record have occurred since 1981 and that 10 of the warmest years on record have occurred during the last 12 years, notwithstanding a solar minimum that occurred from 2007-2009. By using ice cores NASA scientists have determined that carbon monoxide levels had not exceeded 300 parts per million for the last 650,000 years until 1950. Since then they has spiked to 380 parts. And there is no question that larger quantities of CO_2 act as a greenhouse gas, trapping heat in the atmosphere.

Now, you can argue with NASA if you want to, but it has convinced me the world is warming. The fact that the spike in CO_2 and this warming trend coincide with the beginning of the Industrial Revolution convinces me that humans burning fossil fuels is a significant, if not the predominant, contributing factor to this warming.

I am less convinced that we can predict future world temperatures over the next century. It is hubris to think we can predict how natural developments or human developments such as disruptive technologies might radically alter the future. Nonetheless, I think it is prudent to assume we are likely to see warmer temperatures in the future.

But I am also convinced that attempting to address this situation by having the United States unilaterally burn fewer fossil fuels is folly. The United States contributes only about 18 percent of the world's carbon dioxide emissions. If we cut that in half, something that would be a near physical impossibility and catastrophically costly to the U.S. consumer, the effect would barely be measurable. China's CO2 emissions are already a third higher than the United States', and those of other developing countries, like India, are sharply rising.

Those who believe that we can somehow persuade and cajole other countries to stop burning fossil fuels are delusional. The exploitation of fossil fuels has been the cornerstone of the Industrial Revolution, which for the first time in human history has freed millions from deprivation, cold and hunger. That revolution is just now spreading to the rest of the world. In the last two decades, China and India have lifted more people out of poverty than at any other time in human history. And it has been done on the back of burning relatively cheap fossil fuels.

The developing countries are not going to forgo their emergence into the industrial age because of a fear that doing so may affect the climate. Their internal political stability depends on rapidly increasing their citizens' standard of living. Politically speaking, there is no mechanism to agree to, much less enforce, CO2 emission restrictions. It is not going to happen.

All of this is not to suggest we should not be looking at ways to reduce our reliance on fossil fuels. There are other bad side effects from burning fossil fuels that have more immediate harmful effects. It produces emissions that cause smog and fine particulate matter, both of which cause respiratory problems. We also make a lot of useful products out of fossil fuels, and we will run out of the stuff one day. Letting it literally go up in smoke is not a good idea in the long term.

But whatever we do to reduce burning fossil fuels has to make economic sense. The American public is not going to pay dramatically higher energy costs in some quixotic attempt to reduce greenhouse gases.

One reasonable strategy would be to get serious about conservation. And to some degree we have. Per capita energy use in the United States has been falling in recent years. According to a recent study reported in *Scientific American*, our reduction in per capita energy use and a higher reliance on natural gas actually reduced U.S. carbon emissions by nearly 2 percent last year.

And that brings up natural gas. Burning natural gas produces only about half the carbon dioxide other fossil fuels do. While President Obama has paid lip service to developing and exploiting the vast natural gas reserves that have been unlocked with new technologies in the last decade, his administration has actually done more to impede the conversion to natural gas than encourage it. Why we do not have a national policy that encourages and incentivizes the rapid development of natural gas use, especially to replace diesel as a transportation fuel, is beyond comprehension.

But we also need to be thinking about dealing with the consequences of a warmer earth and begin developing strategies to mitigate problems that will cause. The most obvious is that much of the world's population lives along the coasts in relatively low-lying areas. We need to be thinking about how to protect those areas from a rising sea level.

But instead of any of these, the Obama administration and many environmentalists have blinders on and can see no solution except trying to reduce carbon emissions by burning fewer fossil fuels. Primarily they seek to accomplish this by jiggering the market to make green energy, like wind and solar, more competitive. This strategy is enormously expensive and is subject to crony capitalism and other unintended consequences. But most important, it will not, at the end of the day, have any significant effect on climate change.

February 4, 2013

GOVERNMENT DYSFUNCTION

*O*ne of the principal reasons our country has been unable to address the issues discussed in the previous
chapter is the partisan dysfunction into which we
have devolved.

*There are many possible explanations for the atmosphere
of hyper-partisanship that exists today, but I have come to
believe that our current electoral system is largely to blame.*

*The columns in this section address this problem and oth-
er dysfunctions in our political life.*

Impossible Dream

I had a wonderful dream the other night that there was a third U.S. political party, the Independent Moderates. Their candidates did not appear on cable news programs, incessantly repeating talking points at ever-increasing decibel levels. Instead they actually discussed substantive issues and conceded there are almost always two sides to every issue. They even expressed the heretical view that well-intentioned, intelligent people might see issues differently and that it was possible to disagree on policy issues without accusing the other side of treachery or stupidity.

The Independent Moderates were running on a platform that called for ending our dependence on foreign oil as the highest national security priority and declared it imperative that the nation pursue all forms of alternatives, at least until one or more was proved to be technologically superior.

They believed that the U.S. should always have the strongest military in the world but that it should be used judiciously.

They believed that reducing our carbon emissions was important but that without international cooperation our nation's efforts would be largely symbolic. They also recognized that the transition to a noncarbon-based energy stream would be a long, difficult process and that the country could commit economic suicide by setting unrealistic timetables.

They believed that every generation should pay its own bills and that the government should not borrow money except to build long-term infrastructure assets. They believed that neither unfettered nor government-dominated markets were realistic and that our long-term economic prosperity depended on striking a reasonable balance between these two extremes.

They saw immigration as one of our country's great strengths and heritages but believed that our immigration laws should be both reasonable and enforced. They believed that we should stop pretending that deporting 10 million people was a realistic option and should come up with a plan to deal fairly with those who came here illegally while our system was broken.

They believed that education is critical for the country's future but that local communities do not really need the direction of the federal or state governments in deciding how our children should be educated.

They believed that the complexity of the Internal Revenue Code is a national embarrassment and that exemptions and rates should be reduced. They believed that the income tax should be progressive but not to the extent that success is penalized.

They believed that every American should have access to a basic level of health care and be protected from the financial disaster of a catastrophic illness. They also believed that individuals who engaged in unhealthy lifestyle choices such as smoking or obesity should pay a health insurance premium that reflects the costs of those choices. They believed that mental health is as critical as physical health and that our fundamentally broken mental health system needs to be fixed.

They believed that faith is an important part of our national character but not part of our government. They believed that faith leaders should spend more time trying to change hearts than laws.

They believed that a woman has a right to control her own body but are troubled by the dramatic increases in abortions in the last several decades. They believed that if a woman becomes pregnant, she loses the right to terminate that pregnancy at some point during the development of the fetus. They conceded that there was no bright line on when that right was forfeited but were prepared to support the Supreme Court's demarcation of the first trimester. They believed that society should do a better job of supporting mothers who elect to keep their babies.

They believed in the right to bear arms but also in the right to be protected from mentally ill people having guns.

In short, they believed that driving the middle of road was best and that by going too far left or right the country would end up in the ditch.

Unfortunately, my dream ended when I woke and groggily reached for the remote to turn on the morning news. When I joined a program in progress that featured two members of Congress, one from each of our fine political parties, screaming at each other over the issue *du jour*, I realized my dream was over and I had returned to the nightmare of our current vitriolic, hyperpartisan reality.

June 26, 2014

No Place to Call Home

L et me say at the outset that I am extremely reluctant to even use the words "conservative" or "liberal." Both words have been so bastardized that they have almost no meaning. It used to be that if you were conservative you believed that traditional political and social approaches had worked well and should be maintained. It did not mean you had to pass litmus-paper tests on a menu of social issues that bordered on a belief in a theocracy. It used to be that to be liberal meant you believed in utilizing new, progressive methods of approaching social and political problems. It did not mean you subscribed to a blind faith in social welfare programs, regardless of the fact that the programs were driving the bodies politic into bankruptcy.

But to the extent those terms have any contemporary meaning, I and many of my friends find ourselves generally supporting conservative fiscal principles but feeling more liberal on social issues. Perhaps "libertarian" would be a better word than "liberal" because the sentiment is more about government needing a compelling justification to start telling me what I can and cannot do. But if you believe both that Roe v. Wade should not be overturned and that the federal government needs to balance its budget, you have no political home in today's bifurcated partisan political landscape.

I do not think that I am alone in feeling disaffected in the current bipolar political dynamic. A number of organizations and even some third parties have recently been formed seeking to provide an alternative.

I recently spoke to a young lady who was involved in the organization of a third party known as the Moderate Party in Rhode Island's 2010 elections. What the party's name lacked in originality was made up in large measure by its motto, "Fiscally Responsible, Socially Tolerant."

It describes very much my sentiments while avoiding the confusion attending the politically charged terms of "conservative" or "liberal."

Unfortunately the Moderate Party had modest success. It polled only a little more than 6 percent in the Rhode Island governor's race, but that was enough to secure it a place on the ballot in the next election. Interestingly, the governorship was won by Lincoln Chafee, an independent. Chafee and the Moderate Party candidate together polled more than 42 percent of the vote, 10 points ahead of the Republican candidate and 20 points ahead of the Democratic candidate.

Still, it is not easy to break the Democratic/Republican partisan oligarchy. The two dominant political parties have laced the elections statutes with provisions that stack the deck against third-party or independent candidates. For example, in Texas an independent candidate must collect about 50,000 signatures to get on the November ballot and the petitioners cannot have voted in the primary, a daunting task to say the least.

But it seems likely that the current dissatisfaction with the contemporary political landscape so dominated by bipolar extremism will find some form of expression. Whether that takes the form of the rise of a third party, more independent candidates or a repositioning of one of the two dominant parties, I cannot predict. But the great middle of America has time and again served as ballast for our ship of state, keeping her from listing too far to port or starboard. The challenge this time around will be to see if it can keep the ship from splitting apart.

I will make one prediction, however. I predict that about an equal number of readers will write in to respond to this column accusing me of being either a RINO (Republican-In-Name-Only) or a closet liberal Democrat, for those on the far extremes cannot imagine there is an authentic American middle.

I also predict they will ultimately be proved wrong.

May 30, 2011

Tyranny of Minorities

Watching the shameful spectacle in our nation's capital masquerading as a national government, I cannot help but be reminded of George Washington's dire warning about political parties. In his Farewell Address to the nation, Washington forcefully warned the country that "political parties serve to organize faction, to give it an artificial and extraordinary force; to put, in the place of the delegated will of the nation the will of a party, often a small but artful and enterprising minority of the community [resulting in] ill-concerted and incongruous projects ... they are likely ... to become potent engines, by which cunning, ambitious, and unprincipled men will be enabled to subvert the power of the people and to usurp for themselves the reins of government .... "

I cannot imagine a more prescient description of the sorry state of affairs in which we now find our country.

Since World War II, federal expenses and revenues have averaged about 20 percent and 18 percent of gross domestic product, respectively, leaving an average deficit of about 2 percent. But since 2009, expenses have gone up to 25 percent of GDP, and revenues have fallen to 15 percent, resulting in an unsustainable deficit of 10 percent of GDP. Expenses at 25 percent of GDP are at their highest level since World War II. Revenues at 15 percent of GDP are the lowest since World War II. It is beyond absurd to think that at these extremes expenses should not be cut or that revenues should not be increased.

What makes the situation even more infuriating is that 70 percent to 80 percent of Americans have already concluded that the federal deficit should be reduced by cutting expenses a lot and raising taxes a little. It is a common-sense approach that would put us in line with historical levels of federal expenses and revenues and return us to a sustainable financial path.

Why is it, then, that Congress continues to defy the will of the American people to return to historical levels of revenues and expenses? It is actually pretty simple. The minority of Americans who believe that the deficit should be solved either by solely cutting expenses or raising taxes are the voters who dominate the primaries of the Democratic and Republican parties. It is these voters who continue to give us nothing but ideologues, incapable of compromise, from which to choose in the November elections.

It is past time for the American people to rise up and end this tyranny of the politically extreme minorities. We need reform that breaks the political parties' hold on the election process. We need to make it easier for candidates to run for office without being affiliated with a political party, and we need more people who are willing to stand up and run as independent candidates. We need current officeholders to show us they love this country more than they love their political party, and if not we need to be prepared to fire them.

In the early days of the country, it was politically incorrect to be associated with a political party. Largely due to Washington's view of political parties, almost all of the early candidates, publicly at least, eschewed any connection to political parties. Any hint that a candidate was associated with a political party could cause that candidate to lose the election. It was a far cry from today's situation, where it is almost impossible to get elected without being a true-blue believer in one of the partisan ideologies.

To get any meaningful change in the current system, we are going to have to return to the Founders' view of political parties and start thinking differently about them. Instead of being proud to be associated with a political party, it should be an embarrassment. After this week's debacle with the so-called supercommittee, that sentiment should not be much of a stretch.

November 23, 2011

Two Irreconcilable Camps?

A couple of weeks ago, *The New York Times* columnist Paul Krugman wrote that while he applauded the current calls for a more civil political discourse, he feared it would only have limited efficacy because America consisted of two irreconcilable moral camps. In Krugman's view, America is divided between those whom he characterized as people who believe "they can keep what they earn" and those who believe that "society's winners" should be "taxed to pay for a social safety net." Both Krugman's logic and view of Americans are deeply flawed.

First, for many Americans it is not a question of keeping what they earn, it is a question of spending as they see fit. The notion that society's winners are sitting around hoarding their wealth and ignoring their fellow citizens in need is nonsense. Last year, in the throes of the worst recession in decades, Americans gave away $300 billion to charities. There is no telling how much more was given privately to friends and family members in need. It is possible for us to help those in need without cycling our dollars through the hands of bureaucrats, especially since some of us have noticed that not all of the money seems to get recycled when we choose that mode of distribution.

The question is not whether there should be a social safety net for our fellow Americans. The question is how extensive should it be and what is the proper role of government versus private groups in providing the safety net. Far from being two polar opposites, the question is one of an infinitely nuanced continuum.

Krugman analogizes the current debate over the social safety net to the debate over abortion, an issue that he concludes the country has made no progress in resolving. But in fact the issue has been largely resolved. For a number of years now, the polls indicate that a solid majority of Americans think that abortion is morally wrong but are unwilling to use the police power of the state to enforce their view except in the case of late-stage abortions. In fact, the polls show support growing slowly for this middle ground. There are certainly those on either end of this issue's spectrum that would like to see either all abortions criminalized or abortions available on demand with no restrictions. But the vast middle of the country that provides our civic ballast has and likely will continue to reject these extremes.

There are two reasons Krugman and others are led to the conclusion that America is divided into two camps with no middle ground. First is the cable news media circus that passes as journalism. Every time I tune to Fox or MSNBC, I know that Walter Cronkite must be rolling over in his grave. To stage their theater, the cable news networks inevitably invite the most extreme spokespersons for the issue *du jour*. When is the last time you saw a commentator representing the moderate or independent view?

The second cause for this distorted view of America is our dysfunctional electoral system. The über-gerrymandering, made possible in the last several decades by the computer, and the partisan primary system have guaranteed that the polar extremes will be overrepresented in our elected officials. As a result, it is easy to understand how someone listening to our elected representatives could be misled to believe that their extreme views actually represent us. They do not.

James Carville has said that the great strength of America is that the vast majority of Americans have a very similar vision for what we want this country to be. The disagreements tend to be on how we realize that vision. While Carville shares many of Krugman's political views, their grasp of the American people could not be more different.

America is fundamentally a centrist country, perhaps leaning slightly to the right. Contrary to Krugman's prediction, we are not in for an interminable stalemate of two fundamentally opposing moral views. We will muddle through as we have for the last two-plus centuries, getting it wrong sometimes, but mostly getting it right eventually. We will not turn our backs on our fellow Americans in need nor will we turn over every dollar we make to bureaucrats to decide how to spend for us.

Our forefathers set out to form a more perfect union. It is a work in progress.

February 2, 2011

The Rule

A couple of months ago, a special task force for the city of Houston concluded that the city has been running a structural deficit for the better part of a decade. More daunting was its prediction that the cumulative deficit for the next 20 years would be at least $1 billion and might swell to as much as $11 billion.

The task force identified escalating pension and health care costs as the principal drivers of the looming deficits and made a number of recommendations for trimming those costs. In an op-ed responding to the report, the head of one of the pension funds criticized the report because it concentrated too heavily on the problems with the pension plans and did not investigate "wasteful" spending by the city. The pension official did not give any specific examples of wasteful spending by the city.

One of our local bloggers, Charles Kuffner, posted an entry regarding the pension official's comments about wasteful spending. In response, he said he was adopting the following rule. "If you claim there is wasteful spending, but then fail to say what spending in particular is wasteful, I'm not going to take you seriously. Crying 'waste' is the easiest and laziest dodge in the book. If you're not giving specifics, you're not contributing."

I frequently find myself differing with Kuffner on public policy issues, but on this point I am with him to the molecule. The catch phrase we so often hear is "waste, fraud and abuse." Every candidate promises to ferret it out. And virtually every public official claims to have already done so.

I certainly am not suggesting there is not plenty of waste, fraud and abuse in government. But waste and abuse are often in the eye of the beholding special interest group. One person's waste and abuse is another person's critical program. And after spending more than 30 years around government, my impression is that there is much less outright fraud than the average person may suspect. But regardless of the actual level of waste, fraud and abuse in government, Kuffner's rule is still a good one. Unless you can tell me a specific expenditure you intend to eliminate, don't waste my time.

I would expand the "I am not taking you seriously" rule to those who keep telling us that they want to lower tax rates through broadening the base by eliminating tax "loopholes." As with waste, one person's tax loophole is another person's critical tax policy, typically not just benefiting the proponent's special interest but also saving the entire country from economic ruination.

This is the biggest issue I have with Paul Ryan's "Roadmap for America's Future." There is much to be admired in the fact that Ryan and the House Republicans have laid out the financial dilemma facing the country over the next several decades in plain language. Many of their proposals make sense and in some ways track the findings of the Simpson-Bowles Commission.

But a cornerstone of the Roadmap is a broadly based and dramatic reduction in income tax rates. The Roadmap authors say the revenue lost by lowering the rates will be made up by eliminating tax loopholes. However they do not say which ones.

The problem is that the largest deductions are very popular. The largest—constituting more than two-thirds of all tax deductions—are:

- The exclusion of employer-paid health insurance.

- Home mortgage deduction.
- Lower rates for capital gains and dividends (I'm pretty sure this is not one the Republicans are thinking about eliminating).
- The exclusion of Medicare benefits.
- The exclusion of contributions to pension plans.
- The earned income tax credit for low-income filers.
- The deduction for state and local taxes.
- Charitable deductions.
- The exclusion of capital gains on death.

Of course, the reason Republicans have not specified any particular deduction for elimination is that there is a large constituency supporting each of them. If there were not, they would have never found their way into the tax code in the first place.

Generally speaking, the idea of lowering tax rates and broadening the base is a good one. It was a concept specifically endorsed by the Simpson-Bowles Commission. But unless you are prepared to tell us which deduction you are going to eliminate, I am invoking Kuffner's rule, and I am not going to take you seriously.

May 9, 2012

What Candidates Aren't Saying

I have had the opportunity now to sit through a number of debates and forums and meetings with this paper's editorial board for candidates running for the city offices in November. What has amazed me is the lack of discussion of some of the serious challenges facing this city.

For example I have not heard a single candidate say anything about the city's outdated and poorly maintained wastewater collection and treatment system. Unlike many other cities, Houston's wastewater treatment system is highly decentralized. For example while Dallas is only about half Houston's size and population, it still has only two wastewater treatment plants compared to Houston's 40. As a result our system is very costly and difficult to maintain.

The city has also had problems for years with broken sewer lines and the treatments overflowing in heavy rainstorms. These problems contribute to the high bacteria count normally found in the area's bayous and make the city one of the region's worst polluters. Houston has been under pressure from the Texas Commission on Environmental Quality for years to clean up its act on wastewater. There is not even an ongoing discussion about how we could improve the system.

Almost none of the candidates has mentioned air quality. That has been particularly ironic because the backdrop for the last several editorial board meetings has been a brown haze hugging the horizon just outside the Chronicle's windows. While the city has a limited role to play in air quality, it nonetheless is an issue that should at least be on the candidates' agendas.

Not a single person has mentioned that we are spending less on parks than we were 10 years ago. In 2002 the Parks Department budget was $91 million. It got up to a high of $103 million in 2008 but has declined every year since. If you adjust for inflation, it means we are actually spending about 25 percent less on parks today than we were in 2002. The story is pretty much the same for the library budget.

Only a few candidates have recognized that the city's population growth has apparently ground to a halt while the growth in that portion of Harris County outside the city has continued to explode. According to the city's website its population grew from 1,953,000 in 2000 to 2,151,000 in 2013. That is about 10 percent in 13 years, less than 1 percent annually. During the same time period, the population of Harris County outside the City of Houston went from just under 1.5 million to over 2.1 million, a nearly 50 percent increase.

Even on the issues that the candidates do discuss, there is little comprehensive understanding or any plan of action. For example crime comes up in virtually every discussion. But almost none of the candidates seems to know that the crime rate in Houston, following the national trend, has been falling dramatically for the last couple of decades. Frequently, you will hear a candidate say we need more police officers on the street or greater funding for the police department, notwithstanding that we have more than doubled the budget in just the last few years and that study after study shows there is almost no correlation between the number of officers in a department and the crime rate.

By this time almost everyone recognizes the city has some long-term financial challenges driven mostly by its pension systems, but only a handful of candidates seem to understand that we have balanced the city's budget for the last 10 years by failing to fund the pensions with the amount the actuaries say is necessary to pay benefits already earned, thus in essence borrowing from the pensions. Nor do many of the candidates realize the city will almost certainly become technically insolvent in the next couple of years.

One would hope that if a person is going to spend the time and resources it takes to stand for one of the city's offices, he or she would also devote the time to understand the most serious issues facing the city and develop plans to address them. But sadly, based on what I have heard from the candidates, that is largely not the case.

October 12, 2013

Failure of Term Limits

S ome members of the Houston City Council and other community leaders are once again suggesting it is time we look at updating the city charter. It is a suggestion that is hard to argue with.

The charter is a miserably antiquated document. For example, it contains extensive regulation of dance halls. And there are numerous other provisions regulating mundane topics that would be better left to ordinances. It is also a mish-mash of provisions that overlap and are frequently inconsistent, such as the competing revenue caps passed in 2005. So, there is little doubt the city could benefit by taking a look at scrapping the entire charter and starting from scratch.

But the principal impetus behind the current move to revamp the charter is to re-examine the city's term limits. These provisions currently limit a person to serving three two-year terms in any particular city office.

On the surface, term limits seem to be a good idea. Bring in new blood periodically. Keep city offices from falling into the hands of "professional politicians" and officials from becoming entrenched in their offices through the power of incumbency.

But term limits clearly have not worked. Instead, they have produced a succession of administrations and councils focused on short-term issues (and, frequently, the next political office) and more than willing to kick the hard, long-term problems down the road to the next administration and council.

Since Houston adopted term limits in 1991, it has become one of the worst-managed cities in the country, at least from a financial standpoint. A comparison prepared by controller candidate Bill Frazer, who is a certified public accountant, shows that Houston's net assets (roughly equivalent to the city's net worth) have declined faster in the last 10 years than any major city other than Chicago. That's right, believe it or not, even faster than Detroit. Meanwhile, many other cities, such as Los Angeles, Phoenix and Atlanta, have increased their net assets.

And just about everyone agrees that the city will become technically insolvent in the next two to three years. Houston's net unrestricted assets—that is, those assets that are not earmarked for a particular purpose—are already at a $2.2 billion deficit. The city's total debt has ballooned in the last 10 years by more than 80 percent. A recent analysis by Moody's ranks Houston as fifth in the country in terms of its pension expense relative to its budget.

City officials are quick to lay the blame for the city's poor financial performance on external factors, such as the 2008-2009 recession. And, certainly, there have been a number of challenges.

But it was possible for the city to manage through these challenges without squandering its financial reserves. We know that is true because just across downtown, Harris County, operating in the same economic environment, did just that.

Unlike the city, the county's net assets have increased over the last 10 years. Its debt has grown at a much slower pace. Its annual pension cost is $75 million compared to the city's $370 million, even though it has two-thirds as many employees. And its unfunded pension liability at approximately $450 million is a fraction of the city's crippling burden. Nor has the county issued any of the disastrous pension obligation bonds while the city has obligated its taxpayers for more than $600 million.

While there are many structural differences between the city and the county, the lack of term limits for the Commissioners Court is the most glaring. When a person is elected to Commissioners Court, the likelihood is that he or she will serve for an extended period.

Most recently, commissioners have served for decades, although as Commissioner Sylvia Garcia discovered, the voters can decide to make a change.

This kind of longevity has its own drawbacks, but at least it tends to encourage long-term financial stability. If you are going to be around when the bills come due, you are more likely to be concerned about the ability to pay them.

There are many reasons to have a charter commission look at drafting a new city charter. Re-examining terms limits is one of those.

October 5, 2013

Open Primaries Deserve a Look

A number of states are considering or have already adopted various versions of the open primary system (also referred to as a "nonpartisan blanket" or "jungle" primary). The common feature of the various open primary systems is a single primary in which all candidates appear on the same ballot. The top two vote getters, regardless of party affiliation, advance to the general election. The theory behind the open primary system is that it creates the possibility of a November election with two candidates from the same party. In that case, even in districts that have been severely gerrymandered to favor one party, a more moderate candidate would have a chance of winning the seat.

One of the criticisms leveled against the open primary system is that it disadvantages third-party candidates because it is unlikely that a third-party candidate would finish in first or second place. As a result, third parties would rarely be represented on the November ballot. However, if a third-party candidate cannot muster enough votes to come in second in the primary, there would be little chance of that candidate winning in the general election. Also, most of the open primary systems have more liberal rules for candidates gaining a place on the primary ballot, actually making it more likely that third parties would have some ballot representation.

Also on the plus side is that an open primary would nearly eliminate the benefits received from the recent flurry of both Republican and Democratic candidates lending support to third-party candidates to attempt to game the electoral system, an electoral version of "the enemy of my enemy is my friend." One of the most callous of examples of this tactic was the recruitment of street people to stand as candidates for the Green Party by Republican operatives in Arizona.

This tactic is effective because House and Senate seats are elected by plurality in the general election.

For example, if Republican candidates can siphon off votes from their Democratic opponents by ensuring a Green Party candidate is on the ballot (a la Arizona), it increases that candidate's chances of winning a plurality. The same is true if a Democratic candidate were to recruit or assist a Libertarian or tea party candidate to take votes away from a Republican candidate.

This tactic is quickly becoming popular with both sides. In addition to the Arizona shenanigans, in the current election for Pennsylvania's 7th Congressional District, accusations have recently surfaced that supporters of the Democratic candidate assisted the tea party candidate in collecting the necessary petitions to gain a spot on the ballot. A host of other similar allegations have been made, and who knows how many such schemes have gone undetected?

In the last century, U.S. Senate seats have been decided by a plurality in more than 140 elections. And if you do not think that such an electoral scenario can have a dramatic effect, consider Harry Reid's 1998 election. Reid won that election with 48 percent of the vote. He defeated his Republican opponent by 421 votes. In that election the Libertarian party candidate received a little more than 8,000 votes. Given the predispositions of most Libertarian voters, it seems likely they would have voted for Reid's Republican opponent if no Libertarian candidate had been on the ballot in 1998. In an open primary system, it is likely that Reid would not have been elected and, therefore, would never have become the Senate majority leader. Given your own partisan leaning you may think that would have been a good or bad result. But the probability that the open primary system would affect elections is hard to doubt.

An open primary system would allow all parties and independent candidates to have an opportunity to more easily appear on a ballot. It would also assure that the winner is elected by a majority of the voters participating in the election with the largest turnout. At the same time it would effectively eliminate the benefits from gaming the system by aiding third-party candidates in an attempt to prevent their opponents from garnering a majority. All things considered, it seems vastly superior to the current system, which continues to produce more and more ideologically driven office holders.

September 15, 2010

Misplaced Priorities

A couple of weeks ago, I was docked at the 79th Street Boat Basin in New York City. The facility is owned and maintained—and I use that term loosely—by the city of New York.

The boat basin is located where West 79th Street runs into the Hudson River. As you might imagine, it is a spectacular location. Beautiful skyline, a subway station a couple of blocks away, the Museum of Natural History and Lincoln Center within easy walking distance, great restaurants and delis located nearby.

There is only one problem: The place is a dump. An overworked staff struggles to keep the place from completely falling apart. The docks are rickety with numerous makeshift repairs. Only a few of the electrical outlets worked. One had caught fire sometime in the past and had not been replaced. It seemed to be such a waste of an incredible location and municipal asset.

But the saddest was a handrail. And it was not just any handrail. All along that portion of the Hudson River is Riverside Park. It runs for several miles. And along nearly the entire length is a guardrail that keeps people from falling into the Hudson.

For at least the couple of miles that I walked along this guardrail, it was topped with a teak handrail. It was about six inches wide and more than two inches thick. The handrail had been milled from solid teak boards into an oval cross-section. Each piece had been carefully fitted together with diagonal joints, and the connecting hardware was hidden with carved teak plugs. It should have been stunningly beautiful. If you have seen the teak woodwork on boats, you know what I am talking about.

But this was not stunningly beautiful because apparently nobody had touched the handrail since it had been installed. The problem with teak is that if you leave it exposed, its surface quickly oxidizes and turns a dull gray color. So instead of a gorgeous teak handrail along the Hudson, you see an ugly-to-nondescript one.

I cannot even imagine what it would cost to re-create that handrail today. The last time I looked, teak was running something over $20 per board-foot, so just the materials for a handrail several miles long would run into the millions. And that is before the labor and equipment to mill and fit it.

It is not rocket science to maintain teak. It takes some elbow grease and some varnish. It is something just about anybody can do.

Consider that along with the fact that the unemployment rate in New York City is more than 8 percent. There are nearly 800,000 people receiving unemployment benefits in New York state and more than 300,000 on welfare in the city.

Something is wrong with this picture. We have hundreds of thousands of people apparently with time on their hands who are receiving support from the government; the government has a depreciating asset that needs maintenance. How can our government be so dysfunctional as not to be able to match up people looking for something to do with work that needs to be done?

And I don't mean to pick on New York. I could say the same thing about abandoned lots in Houston that need to be mowed, or litter along the freeways or hundreds of other things that just need a little sweat equity.

There was one other interesting contrast evident during my stay at the Boat Basin. Docked immediately next to me was a brand new, gleaming 30-foot rigid inflatable Homeland Security patrol boat. It had four gigantic outboard engines and all kinds of bells and whistles. It had to have set the U.S. Department of Homeland Security back upward of a half-million dollars.

However, during the week I was there, it never left the slip. In fact, no one even came to check on it that I saw. You have to wonder over the life of that boat—which in those conditions will only be a few years—if it will ever serve any useful purpose. Yet, somehow we find the money for fancy patrol boats but not to maintain a multimillion dollar teak handrail.

What does that say about our priorities?

August 3, 2013

AMERICA'S PLACE
IN A CHANGING WORLD

*I*n America we have established the world's first post-tribal nation, based not on geographic or ethnic identification but on ideals of freedom, self-governance, and constitutional limits on the will of the majority. It has been a fabulously successful experiment. So much so that notwithstanding the Soviet Union's brief challenge to American hegemony, since World War II the United States has set the table for world affairs.

But the world is rapidly changing. Countries like China have borrowed parts of our formula and are now eager to take their place on the world stage. Other countries, like many in the Middle East, continue to be plagued by tribal hatreds and feuds that spill over into the rest of the world.

As with our domestic challenges there is no simple course by which to navigate the world's rapidly changing dynamics. In my columns on foreign affairs I have tried to apply the same formula, setting aside cultural biases and looking hard at the facts on the ground and their implications for our country.

Complexities of Foreign Policy

L ast year I was invited to a dinner with some retired Chinese diplomats who were touring the United States. Henry Kissinger's new book on China had recently come out, so I decided to grab a copy and bone up before the dinner. As I began reading the book, it soon became apparent I had grossly underestimated both how long it would take to read Kissinger's 500+-page tome and my own ignorance of Chinese culture and history. I ended up having time to scan only the first hundred pages or so.

The five-hour, 117-course dinner (just kidding, it was really only about 10 courses) was an eye-opening experience. Our hosts had been high-ranking diplomats in the Chinese Foreign Service and were exceedingly well-educated and articulate. As the dinner wore on, two things became increasingly apparent to me. First, and the more encouraging, was how similar were the aspirations we each held for our countries and the world generally. Less encouraging, or perhaps more daunting would be a better description, were the differences in our views on the current state of the world based on vastly different cultural and historical experiences.

The dinner inspired me to complete a detailed reading of Kissinger's book along with a good many other materials on China. This was also toward the end of the Republican presidential primary in which much of the campaigning had been based on China bashing, with the likes of Donald Trump leading the charge. What my limited study of China quickly taught me is that neither a political campaign nor the popular media could ever capture the complexity of that country and our relationship to it.

For example, there is a great deal of discussion and concern among the neo-cons about China's expansionary intents. But while China has long referred to itself as an empire, it has never carried out a colonial policy in the manner of the British or Roman empires. It has occupied roughly the same territory for about 5,000 years. On only one occasion did it have a substantial navy, and after an extended voyage in the 1400s, destroyed it, concluding it had no value.

Rather, China has been obsessed for millennia with its perimeter security. Imagine if the United States were surrounded on three sides with a dozen or more countries that periodically decided they would like to have some of our land and resources. It is China's ever-shifting alliances and conflicts with her immediate neighbors that have dominated Chinese strategic thinking, not expanding some vast empire.

But this strategic subtlety is something almost impossible to convey in the popular media or in a presidential debate. When you multiply this simple example by hundreds of other complexities in the Sino-American relationship, and then that times the hundreds of relationships we have with other countries in the world, you quickly realize how ill-suited our modes of public policy debate are when addressing the complexities of foreign policy. It also makes apparent how sophomoric and potentially damaging Trump-like demagoguing of foreign policy issues is, especially in the context of a presidential campaign.

I think our Founding Fathers grasped that foreign relations was a democracy's weak point when they vested most of the authority over foreign affairs in the executive branch.

In the hundreds of hours I have spent reading about China in the last year, I have achieved only the most rudimentary understanding of that country and our relationship with it. Some other areas of the world, for example the Middle East, are arguably even more complex. The truth is that the average person has neither the time nor the inclination to become versed on the complexities of our foreign relations.

And I think that is something important to remember the next time some snake-oil salesman masquerading as a politician or a talk show host starts telling you, for example, that all of U.S. unemployment problems stem from China's currency manipulations. There may be a grain of truth to some of these narratives, but the reality is always, *always*, more complex and more nuanced than the dribble you get on talk shows or political debates.

March 22, 2013

Russians Being Russians

Time and again I see the American public and even some of our foreign policymakers attempt to interpret the actions of other nations through the prism of our national experience. It is almost always a mistake because our national experience is unlike any other country's on Earth.

It is especially the case when we attempt to divine the actions and motives of Russia and China. These ancient countries have a history many years older than ours. It causes them to see the world in starkly different terms than do we.

Both countries have been around in one form or another for thousands of years. Their ancestors have lived in more or less the same geographic areas for hundreds of generations. And both countries have been forced to defend borders thousands of miles long against mostly hostile neighbors for their entire histories. In China's case, they have been literally surrounded for their entire history.

Both have been the victims of bloody invasions and internal anarchy. Each has lost millions of their people from wars with their neighbors and civil wars. It should hardly be a surprise that we find them obsessed with security, both internal and external.

Take just the most recent case of Russia's involvement in World War II. By most accounts, Russia lost more than 20 million people in that war. They suffered more than twice the number of casualties that Germany suffered, even though Germany lost the war. They had more than 40 times the casualties of the United States. There was hardly a

Russian family that did not lose a member to that bloody conflict.

As Americans, we have no similar experience. If we had lost a similar share of our population in World War II, our casualties would have been around 15 million, the equivalent of losing every person living in New York, Chicago and Los Angeles. It is hard to even imagine what that kind of catastrophe would have done to our national psyche.

And that is just the most recent memory. The Russians have fought wars with the Ottomans, Japanese, Mongolians, Persians, Swedes and, of course, most famously Napoleon's French. And most of these were fought on their soil. We should hardly find it surprising if they are a little paranoid about border security.

When you come from that kind of historical perspective, diplomats waving international law treatises and threats of economic sanctions are so much tissue. And this history also shows that the suggestion the Russians would not have taken this action had President Obama pursued a hard-line strategy is utter nonsense.

Recognizing this reality is not to condone Russia's current annexation of Crimea. But to think that Russia is suddenly going to conform to international law instead of reacting to what it sees as a potential threat to its security, i.e. a westward-leaning Ukraine, is naive in the extreme. A couple thousand years of history suggest otherwise.

Nor does a recognition of Russia's historical perspective suggest that the United States and Europe should not exact a price for Russia's action. But that should be and will be limited to diplomatic and economic sanctions. No one is going to war for the cause of Ukrainian versus Russian administration of Crimea.

In the end, Russia may well regret its annexation of Crimea. The place is an economic basket case. Some estimates suggest that Russia will have to pump $3 billion annually into Crimea to keep it afloat.

One of the problems Russia will inherit, one that Houstonians can sympathize with, is billions in unfunded pensions promised by the Ukrainian government. Russia also will have to manage the unruly Tartar minority and rebuild infrastructure neglected by the previous corrupt Ukrainian administrations.

And Russia already has its hands full. Its economy is sluggish at best. Because of shale drilling technology, it is facing new competition for its principal petroleum products. And it is already saddled with supporting the Syrian government in its civil war and with an ongoing internal terrorist threat from several ethnic groups. Putin may be repeating the same mistake of over-reaching ambitions as his Soviet predecessors.

We must hope that the United States will manage this crisis in a way that exacerbates Russia's cost of going rogue without precipitating an outright military conflict. It can be an opportunity for the United States to build closer economic and diplomatic ties to Europe and thus further isolate Russia. It should also be used as an opportunity to open up European markets for American LNG and shale drilling technology to develop European fields.

This is a time for smart, opportunistic statecraft, not mindless chest-beating or fanciful entreaties to impotent international legal principles.

March 19, 2014

A Cautionary Sign

A s I watched the shuttle roar flawlessly into outer space on its last mission, I could not help thinking that somewhere an aging Sputnik scientist was gloating, "Comrade, we have beaten you after all." There is something profoundly disturbing to me about the fact that America, the greatest nation on the planet, will not have the capability to put a human into outer space for at least the next five years and will instead have to rely on its old rival to do so.

Don't get me wrong. I am not one of the wingnuts who thinks the country is about to collapse. I am not buying gold, and I don't see socialist conspiracies under every tea leaf.

But watching my country give up its ability to place a human in outer space for the first time in more than four decades and become dependent on Russia made me wonder if American supremacy is on the wane. It made me wonder if America is still capable of doing the big things.

The generation that came before had no such self-doubts. They went from not even being in the space race to placing a man on the moon in barely a decade. They built the interstate highway system, the intercoastal waterway, an incredible network of airports, an unparalleled electrical grid, a higher education system that has attracted thousands from all over the world and countless other big civic undertakings. And they did so while incurring relatively little debt.

Today we cannot seem to do anything but cave in to special interests that line up at the public trough. We are like spoiled children throwing tantrums to get our way and our two political parties like overly indulgent parents only too anxious to give us our candy to shut us up, even if it rots our teeth.

Republicans genuflect to the rich and corporate chieftains promising them ever lower tax rates, notwithstanding that their rates are already the lowest in our lifetimes. Democrats demagogue by demanding higher taxes on the rich and corporations, pretending that will solve our fiscal problems, while continuing to support entitlement programs that a fifth-grader with a pocket calculator can show are fundamentally unsustainable.

In the meantime, our highways and bridges are crumbling. Our power plants and grid are ancient, inefficient and dumb. Our cities' sewer systems have surpassed industry as the most serious polluters. Our education system is leaving millions behind, and a college education is increasingly becoming reserved for the rich or those lucky enough to win the scholarship lottery. And don't even get me started on our impotence at becoming energy self-sufficient as a nation.

And as I survey the field of elected officials and candidates, I see few that give me any confidence that they can lead our nation back to doing the big things again. I see many obsessively ambitious for power but few prepared to actually lead. I don't hear them asking us to sacrifice for the good of the country as our forefathers were called upon to do during times of hardship. Instead, they continue to tell us that we can all have our cake and eat it too.

In 1962, when John Kennedy set the audacious goal of going to the moon by the end of the decade, he said we would do it not because it was easy but because it was hard. It is almost impossible today to imagine one of our leaders standing up and asking us to do something hard.

But I should not be too hard on the politicians. After all, they are a reflection of us. We cannot expect our leaders to be different until we are prepared to be different. They will put the interests of the country ahead of their political self-interests when we begin doing it ourselves.

History is replete with examples of great nations or empires that began their decline into oblivion by hiring mercenaries to do their fighting for them. The beginning of the descent of the Roman Empire, the Italian Renaissance city-states and the Spanish Empire coincided with when they began to hire other folks to do the hard things their citizens were not willing to do.

Giving up on manned space flight and hiring the Russians to ferry us into orbit may not be as consequential as the Romans hiring one group of barbarians to protect them from other barbarians, but something about it feels depressingly similar.

July 13, 2011

Unrest Here to Stay

I n recent days reports of protests and violent political upheaval in Venezuela and Ukraine have come in the wake of similar incidents throughout the world during the past four years.

Ever since an obscure merchant in Tunisia set himself on fire as a protest against government corruption and sparked a revolution, the world has been ablaze with indigenous protests and uprisings. A website that chronicles such incidents lists nearly 100 protests in more than 30 countries since 2010. And that does not include the thousands of protests taking place in China, mostly over the government's failure to protect the environment.

So what in the world is going on?

Technology likely is a major contributing cause. Today as never before, the world is tied together with instantaneous communication. Even the most remote Bedouins can now access the New York Times. And they are discovering that a significant fraction of the human race has pulled itself out of the abject poverty and autocratic rule that have dominated the human experience.

We forget what a rarified bubble we live in. Of the roughly 100 billion humans who have walked this Earth, only a tiny fraction have lived in a free society with relative plenty. The overwhelming human experience has been of suffering under the heel of some autocrat and scratching out a subsistence living. And so it is, even today, for much of the world.

But now that anyone, anywhere, can see on satellite television or a smartphone that it is possible to live in a free society, the genie is out of the bottle. And that same technology allows them to connect with each other and organize as never before.

In the long run, this new age of enlightenment will be a good thing for the world. It will lift billions out of poverty and slavery. But in the short run, it is going to be painful. It will come in fits and starts. It will be accompanied by violence, much of it tribal. Revolutions will be hijacked by new, aspiring autocrats and extremists. Nation states will react to beat down the protests when they perceive them as threats to their national interest, as Russia is currently doing in the Ukraine.

And the revolutions will not always be friendly to America. Our spotty record of sometimes pursuing our national self-interest at the expense of promoting local democracies is a legacy that will take some time to live down.

And not all emerging democracies will see their self-interest aligned with ours, nor will they completely share our values.

It will also be frustrating to Americans how little influence we will have over these unfolding events.

Since World War II we have gotten used to setting the table of world order through our overwhelming economic and military dominance. But the same technologies setting these events in motion have also blunted that influence. And after the Iraq and Afghanistan wars, Americans for some time are going to be less enthusiastic about intervening directly in what are mostly internal disputes. We have learned from those wars the costs and limitations of such foreign excursions. For the most part, we will be observers exercising only diplomatic and economic levers.

In the end, either you believe in democracy or you don't. It is not for us to say that some particular group is not ready for self-governance, although, indeed, they may not be. But we must have faith that, notwithstanding how messy this may become in the meantime, the great experiment in self-governance that began on our soil is on its way to being not the exception but the universal condition of all mankind. And that, as our Founding Fathers predicted, will be the great American legacy.

March 5, 2014

Arab Spring and the Islamic Renaissance

Since the decline of the Ottoman Empire during the 16th century, there can be little argument that, by almost any metric, the Islamic countries have fallen behind the rest of the world. For the last several centuries, most Muslims have lived in deplorable economic, social and political circumstances.

There are about as many explanations for this decline as there are historians who have studied the issue. Frequently, critics of Islam will attribute the decline to rigidity and backwardness they contend is endemic to that faith.

However, it is hard to imagine a religion more backward, oppressive and hostile to the advancement of civilization than the medieval Catholic Church. And yet the Italian Renaissance emerged to transform Europe and set off five centuries of Western civilization's hegemony.

But regardless of the reasons for the stagnation, many signs are pointing to a Middle Eastern, and hence, an Islamic, Renaissance.

Of course, the most obvious signs are the recent political revolutions in the Arab world, which have so far deposed three despots and threatened several more. But the changes throughout the Islamic world are actually more fundamental than the political victories in these Arab countries.

In attempting to interpret the Arab Spring, we need to avoid the common misconception of equating Muslims with Arabs. The error is not too surprising, given that Islam originated on the Saudi Arabian peninsula and that the Quran is written in Arabic. However, Arabs make up only about 15 percent of all Muslims worldwide, and the vast majority of Muslims cannot speak Arabic. Indonesia alone has more Muslims than all of the Arab countries combined. So when we talk about the Arab Spring, we must remember that while there may be long-term implications for the rest of the Islamic world, what we are seeing play out in North Africa and the Middle East is more a political than religious phenomenon.

I recently attended a lecture on the rumblings in the Arab world given by Robin Wright, a journalist who has covered the Middle East for four decades. In her new book *Rock the Casbah* Wright documents the growing generational divide in the Arab world that has sparked the current political upheavals. More than a third of Arabs are between 15 and 29 years old. Many of these young people have spent more time on the Internet than they have in a mosque. That exposure to the rest of the world has resulted in seismic social changes, which, until recently, were missed by octogenarian Egyptian generals, American intelligence officials and an aging al-Qaida leadership.

Wright argues that the Islamic generation coming of age today, while observant of their Islamic traditions and heritage, has rejected extremism and violence. The treatment of women has probably been Islam's greatest failing. However, across the Islamic world, a great gender awakening is taking place.

In most Islamic countries, women now make up more than half of the university students. Women Islamic scholars have emerged, challenging male-oriented interpretations of the Quran.

However, we should not interpret this potential renaissance across the Islamic world as being pro-Western. Quite to the contrary, a century of colonial rule and Western support for dictators have left young people ambivalent toward the West.

We also should expect that there will be fits and starts as this movement develops. Certainly revolutions can be hijacked by regressive forces, as occurred in Iran. But we have lived for too long in fear of another Iran.

According to Wright, never in the 1,400 years of Islam have religious authorities actually ruled politically as they do in Iran today. It is a model that is not sustainable over the long term, and there are many indications that it is rapidly becoming unwound.

We cannot afford to be on the wrong side of history in this unfolding drama. Rather than wringing our hands and fretting over this upheaval, we should embrace and celebrate the possibility that 1.5 billion of our fellow humans have a real chance of living freely in democratic societies.

November 16, 2011

Unscrambling the Middle East

S o let me get this straight: Our traditional ally Saudi Arabia is
backing, or at least is sympathetic to, the current insurgents
in Iraq because they are Sunnis. Our traditional enemy Iran,
on the other hand, is backing the same government we support because it is Shiite. But then so is Syrian President Bashar al-Assad,
whom we have pledged to topple because the insurgents in Iraq are
also involved on the opposite side of the civil war in Syria. Add to
this mish-mash: Our strongest ally in the region, Israel, does not get
along with any of these groups. As Hardy would have said to Laurel,
"This is another fine mess you have gotten us into."

As Americans we are used to being able to tell the good guys
from the bad guys. The Nazis were bad guys. The Communists were
bad guys. Just tell us who the bad guys are and we will go kick their
tails. Unfortunately, in the Middle East, there is no such moral clarity,
and it seems we find ourselves mostly trying to pick out who are the
least-bad guys.

On top of the moral ambiguities, there is the matter of 5,000 years
of history between many of these groups, for which we have no comparable cultural analog. The Shia-Sunni schism alone dates back over
a thousand years, three times longer than our country has existed.
And that is only one of the dozens of major rifts in that part of the
world. To make matters even more complicated, and many experts
believe way worse, the nation-state borders were mostly drawn by
Europeans in the early 20th century with little regard to traditional

geographic or cultural boundaries. Also, we fail to grasp that most of the inhabitants of the Middle East have no concept of a pluralistic democracy. One has never existed in their history. I saw an interview of a reporter who had been held captive by the Taliban for seven months. He said his capturers were completely uneducated and most were illiterate. None had ever traveled outside his tribal regions. They believed there was a world war being waged by Christians and Jews to destroy Islam because that was what their leaders had told them.

The concept of a constitutional government that protects the rights of minorities is as alien to them as Sharia law is to us.

Of course in Washington the issue becomes simply part of the partisan blame game. According to the Democrats, it is former President George W. Bush's fault for intervening in the first place. According to the Republicans, it's President Barack Obama's fault for leaving too soon. However, both sides would be well to remember that each president undertook those actions with the strong support of the American people.

America's vacillation between engagement with and retreat from the Middle East is actually part of a larger philosophical conflict that has, from the founding of the republic, marked our foreign policy. On the one hand, there are the practical considerations of what is in our narrow self-interest. This view was summarized in the 19th century by Lord Palmerston, a British foreign secretary and prime minister, when he said, "Nations have no permanent friends or allies; they only have permanent interests."

It is a view similar to that expressed by former President George Washington in his farewell address when he cautioned the country about getting involved in European wars.

But Americans have also seen themselves as something more than a collection of national interests. We have always believed our destiny is to bring democracy and freedom to the entire world. We have always viewed ourselves as the "last, great hope" and a "grand experiment" in self-governance that would show the rest of world the way. Unfortunately, the two views, at least in the short-term, are frequently in conflict, as they are today in the Middle East. Equally unfortunate, there is no simple answer. We are not going to simply drop some bombs and kill a few bad guys and solve all the problems of the Middle East.

Probably the best we can do is to continue to stumble along, feeling our way as we go, trying to do what is right and what is practical. In the final analysis, we must come to accept the limits on our ability to affect outcomes in that part of the world.

June 21, 2014

FAITH, COURAGE, COMPASSION

*T*he kind of society we want, and the individual and collective actions we take to foster it, are grounded in our values. For many of us those values come from our faith traditions.

Many journalists are uncomfortable talking about faith, yet it is one of the most important aspects of our society. It motivates and inspires people and therefore in my estimation cannot be ignored in a discussion of nations and our communities.

Let's Stop Praying in Public

O ur Founding Fathers, fresh from the European experience of mixing the affairs of government and religion and the many evils caused by it, included as the very first clause in the Bill of Rights what has come to be known as the Establishment Clause. The clause prohibits government from setting up a state religion or interfering with people practicing religion as they see fit.

In the early days of the country, the Establishment Clause did not cause much controversy because nearly everyone was a Protestant Christian. The line between church and state was blurred fairly regularly, but because the overwhelming majority of Americans shared similar religious views, no one much objected.

But as Americans became more diverse in their religious faiths, various government practices came under challenge. Ironically, some of the early litigation under the Establishment Clause in the latter part of the 19th century was brought not by atheists but by Catholics objecting to various Protestant practices in public schools.

But it was a series of decisions by the Supreme Court in the early 1960s that declared prayer in public schools to be unconstitutional that set off a cultural war that continues to be waged today. Based on the controversy in recent weeks over a number of different instances of public prayer, we appear to be no closer to resolving this issue than when the Supreme Court handed down those early decisions.

I have a proposal I would like to advance that I think can put this issue to rest once and for all: Let's stop praying in public. Now

I suspect that many religious people may find my suggestion shocking, but I have some pretty good authority for the proposition.

Chapters 5-7 of the Gospel according to Matthew record Jesus' famous Sermon on the Mount. In this sermon, Jesus gives a lesson on praying (see Matthew 6:5-13). At the end of the lesson he gives us a sample prayer, which we now know as the Lord's Prayer and which is probably the most famous passage from the Bible.

However, immediately before the Lord's Prayer, Jesus has some other things to say about prayer that are cited much less frequently:

"And when you pray, do not be like the hypocrites, for they love to pray standing in the synagogues and on the street corners to be seen by others. Truly I tell you, they have received their reward in full. But when you pray, go into your room, close the door and pray to your Father, who is unseen. Then your Father, who sees what is done in secret, will reward you. And when you pray, do not keep on babbling like pagans, for they think they will be heard because of their many words. Do not be like them, for your Father knows what you need before you ask him."

I will concede that there are other Scriptures that, at least inferentially, sanction group or communal prayer. But Jesus' lesson seems at a minimum to admonish us that when we pray, it should be for the purpose of entering a communion with our Creator and not to put on a show for other human beings within earshot.

It is hard for me to see how reading a written prayer over a public-address system at a football game would not more likely fall into that latter category. After all, I am pretty sure the PA system is not being used to make sure God can hear the prayer.

However, I do not want to impugn the motives of those who choose to continue to pray in public, as has recently been done by a number of other commentators. For one of the other lessons from the Sermon on the Mount, and which is similarly more often honored in its breach, is "judge not, lest you be judged."

But I think my proposal is worthy of consideration. It certainly would put to rest a public controversy that has dogged our country for decades. If you are a believer in the Bible, an added benefit would be that we would apparently have a lot more prayers answered. And with all of the challenges our country is facing, I think we all can agree that we could use a few more answered prayers.

August 7, 2011

Difference a Life Can Make

Tomorrow is the birthday of William Wilberforce. Abraham Lincoln once said Wilberforce's name is one that should be known by every schoolboy. Yet I suspect it is one that many of you will not recognize.

Wilberforce was a member of the British Parliament for nearly three decades in the late 1700s and early 1800s. Over his long career in Parliament he enjoyed many accomplishments. But he is best remembered as the person most responsible for the slave trade being outlawed in the British Empire, which proved to be the beginning of the end of legalized slavery throughout the world.

Wilberforce was an unlikely political hero. He was born to a wealthy merchant family and gained admission to St. John's College at Cambridge through his family connections. While he was brilliant, he was more of a *bon vivant* than a serious student throughout his college career. After school, he was elected as one of the youngest members of Parliament.

However, in his mid-20s, Wilberforce experienced a religious conversion. After that he devoted himself to a series of humanitarian causes, abolition being his principal passion. However, he also founded what we now know as the Society for the Prevention of Cruelty to Animals and the Bible Society. He was an early advocate of women's suffrage and the patron of dozens of other charities and causes.

Wilberforce suffered from poor health for most of his life. His health was complicated by addiction to opium, which was an ingredient of laudanum, a medication his physician prescribed. His various afflictions only add to the wonderment at all he accomplished in his life.

Wilberforce was mentored by an Anglican priest named John Newton. Newton was the son of the captain of a slave ship and followed his father into that occupation. By his own accounting, Newton was responsible for the deaths of hundreds of Africans on the passage to the Americas. However, he also experienced a religious conversion and foreswore the slave trade. He wrote the hymn, *Amazing Grace*, about his conversion and devoted the balance of his life to the abolition movement. At several critical junctures, he provided Wilberforce with the encouragement to continue the fight.

There are many lessons to be learned from Wilberforce's life, but perhaps the most salient in today's political climate is about the role of faith in politics. I find politicians disgusting who wear their faith on their sleeves for political advantage. But Wilberforce's faith was the authentic article. It drove his passion for justice and sustained him through many personal and political trials, including his frequent illnesses. His life stands are a sharp rebuttal to those who argue that political leaders must check their faith and the values it represents in the capitol coat closet. It also stands in stark contrast to politicians who show off their faith while not truly standing for the values it teaches.

In 2007 Michael Apted directed a film titled *Amazing Grace*. It is a dramatization of Wilberforce's role in the abolition movement. Watching *Amazing Grace* over the next few days would be a well-deserved tribute to Wilberforce on his birthday and a way to celebrate a remarkable and heroic life that reminds us of the difference that a committed, faithful life can make to rest of the world.

August 22, 2012

What the Bible Says
About Immigrants

A few months ago I was in church listening to our pastor's sermon. He was describing a feast where the prophets had sent out word for all the people of Israel to come together. Interestingly, the invitation to the feast specially included all of the "aliens living among you."

When I got home and I pulled up an electronic version of the Bible and did a search for the word "alien." To my surprise, the search turned up dozens of references. It seems the issue of immigration has been on peoples' minds for some time.

A copy of the passages can be found at www.BillKingHouston.com/scripture. Most are in the Old Testament, and while the message varies, the underlying theme is an admonishment to treat aliens living in your land with tolerance and charity. Frequently, they are grouped with widows and orphans, and the passages charge us with an affirmative duty to see to their well being. In many of these passages, originally written to the Israelites, they are reminded that they will do these things because they once lived as aliens in the land of Egypt.

There are two passages that I found particularly compelling. First is Exodus 12:49:

> *The same law applies to the native-born and to the*
> *alien living among you.*

I am not a big proponent of mixing religion and politics, but I do not believe we should check our faith-based values at the courthouse door or the capitol steps. I find many of the legislative proposals floating around these days pretty inconsistent with this passage.

The second is less legalistic, but even more compelling. Deuteronomy 10:17-19 provides:

> *For the Lord your God is God of gods and Lord of lords, the great God, mighty and awesome, who shows no partiality ... He defends the cause of the fatherless and the widow, and loves the alien, giving him food and clothing. And you are to love those who are aliens, for you yourselves were aliens in Egypt.*

I suppose that those of us who are Christians should not be surprised that the God who commanded us to feed the hungry, attend the sick, cloth the naked and love our neighbors as ourselves would have a similar soft spot for those who have been displaced from their native homeland.

But certainly this passage is hard to reconcile with the rhetoric I have heard from some of my Christian brothers and sisters on this issue. Skeptics are likely to see such inconsistency as hypocrisy, and in many cases I share their skepticism. However, for most I suspect there is a more complicated explanation.

You may be familiar with an Anglican cleric named John Newton, who lived in the latter part of the 18th century. Newton is best known as the composer of what is perhaps the greatest Christian hymn of all time, *Amazing Grace*. Fewer know that Newton began his life as a rogue who fell into the slave trade. Eventually he became captain of a slave ship and by his own account was responsible for the torture and death of many Africans during their transport to the Americas.

Later in his life Newton had a religious conversion—he wrote *Amazing Grace* about that life-changing experience. Eventually he foreswore the slave trade and became an ardent abolitionist, credited with mentoring William Wilberforce, the British member of Parliament who led the successful fight to abolish the slave trade in 1807. But what is more complicated and troubling about Newton's story is that after his conversion he did not immediately give up the slave trade. In fact, after his conversion he captained several more slave trips while living an otherwise pious life.

I think this startling moral inconsistency must be viewed in the context of its social setting. During the last half of the 18th century, other than a few Quakers and Methodists, none of the religious establishment had spoken out against slavery on moral grounds. One can find some Biblical passages that seem to, at least, tolerate the institution, and it had been interwoven into the social fabric of most of the world for millennia. While the diabolic evil of slavery is patently obvious to us today, it was not so for most people in the world at that time.

Today, when good people are confronted with public schools and hospitals pressed beyond capacity, ever rising property taxes to support these institutions, home invasions by criminals in our country illegally, innumerable auto accidents with aliens having no insurance together with a myriad of other problems associated with our broken immigration system, it is hardly surprising that they are frustrated and angry. And unquestionably, these are issues that should be dealt with expeditiously and equitably. After all Exodus says that the *same* laws should apply, not that there should be *no* laws.

However, when I see scenes like a child being torn from its mother because she is being deported or immigrants dying in the back of a truck trying to come to this country to make a better life for themselves and their families, I fear we are suffering from the same moral blindness that Newton did after his conversion but before his epiphany on slavery. I cannot imagine how any Christian can watch families being forcibly separated so that some can be deported and believe that Jesus would approve.

It is said that in the later part of his life Newton memorized the name of every African slave who died in his care and that he daily repeated their names in a prayer seeking forgiveness. Immigration reform is likely to be on the national agenda next year. Some members of the Texas Legislature have indicated there may be some proposals put forth on the state level as well. Certainly there will be many difficult issues in this process on which people of goodwill may honestly disagree. But hopefully we will undertake reforming our system with our faith-based values in mind and not a moral blindness we will one day regret.

December 7, 2008

Robben Island

A few years ago I visited Cape Town, South Africa. All of the tour books said that Robben Island was a must-see for visitors.

Robben Island lies about five miles off the South African mainland, just across from Cape Town's harbor. Before the fall of the apartheid regime, Robben Island was South Africa's Alcatraz. It was where the regime held most of its political prisoners, including Nelson Mandela. For 18 of the 27 years he was imprisoned, he was held at Robben Island. Today, the site is a museum and national monument. I put it on the list of places I would visit while in Cape Town, although I admit not with great enthusiasm. It turned out to be quite more than I expected. Of course I visited the cell where Mandela lived for so many years and was made famous by David Turnley's iconic photograph. But another site, not nearly as well known, had a far greater impact on me: The lime quarry where the government forced prisoners to manually extract that caustic mineral through back-breaking labor in blazing heat.

After Mandela was released from prison and had become the president of South Africa, he visited the quarry with a number of his former inmates. During the visit, Mandela reached down and picked up one of the slag rocks, held it up and said, "This is the rock of South Africa on which we will build a new country."

As he laid down the rock, his fellow former inmates retrieved rocks of their own and laid them down on top of his. That pile of rocks is there to this day, a simple monument to all mankind's yearning to be free. It is impossible to stand at that spot and not be moved by Mandela's struggle. In the wake of the effusive media outpouring surrounding Mandela's death last week, some, mostly in the conservative blogosphere, have criticized mainstream media for overlooking some of Mandela's less-admirable attributes. He struggled with his family life. He flirted with communism and ne'er-do-wells like Libya's Moammar Gadhafi and Cuba's Fidel Castro. And at height of the apartheid conflict, he advocated violence, which caused the United States to place him on the State Department's terrorist list. The truth is that Mandela, like many great men or women, was a complex individual and, in his case, one responding to extreme circumstances.

Who can say what any of us might have done had we been subjected to the type of virulent racism then practiced by the South African government?

It is unfortunate that we tend to want to see our leaders as either all good or all bad, when either is rarely the case. There may be a few pure saints or scoundrels in the ranks, but most are like the rest of us: capable, under the right circumstances, of being both.

There is an old spiritual that you frequently hear at funerals of African-Americans. The title and recurring lyric is: "Let the Work I've Done Speak for Me." It is a good standard for judging a life. And by this test, Mandela must be judged as great. His struggle, albeit along with many other South Africans', created a new democratic country where all are enfranchised—a country where the rights of individuals are respected with an economy based on market principles.

This is not to say that it is some kind of utopia, for it has a long list of challenges and problems, many of which are a hangover from the apartheid era. South Africa's transition was remarkable and especially so considering how little blood was shed in the process. Those who predicted widespread black-on-white violence turned out to be wrong for the most part.

There is no question that Mandela's personal example of forgiveness and reconciliation with his former tormentors was most responsible for the largely peaceful transfer of power. Despite whatever blemishes there may have been on his armor, that work speaks loudest for him and is the reason his life is celebrated by millions this week.

December 11, 2013

The Irreversible Penalty

As a young college student, I was absolutely opposed to the death penalty on moral and public policy grounds.

Fundamentally, it just seemed wrong to me that society should resort to the same violence we were condemning. Also, during that time, we were becoming increasingly aware of how inequitably the death penalty was meted out. I also knew that the deterrent effect of capital punishment has always been muddled at best. There have been a number of high-profile studies claiming a measurable deterrent effect. But those studies have increasingly come under critical attack by other researchers. Also, states without the death penalty consistently have lower murder rates than states with it.

Because murders are so frequently crimes of passion, the deterrent argument never made much sense to me intuitively. Despite their high-profile media coverage, cold-blooded murders, those in which one could argue the murderers might have the presence of mind to be deterred, are actually quite rare. Interestingly, polling shows that the public, notwithstanding its support of capital punishment, has concluded that the death penalty does not provide much of a deterrent.

But when I began studying law and had to read some of the cases that dealt with horrific murders where individuals with little or no motive had senselessly, and sometimes cruelly, taken another person's life, I found myself saying, "I could flip the switch on that guy."

There are some crimes that are so monstrous that the perpetrator has forfeited his right to life. That feeling is the basic human need for retribution. It may not be the most noble of human sentiments, but as the narrative of any melodrama will confirm, it is universal.

But over the years, as I practiced law and tried many lawsuits, I saw how fallible our judicial system is. Don't get me wrong; it is still the best system for determining the truth anyone has devised. But it is far from perfect. So increasingly, I came to realize that if capital punishment continued to be part of our public policy approach to prosecuting criminals, we would undoubtedly from time to time execute an innocent person. In the past couple of decades, the advent of improved DNA evidence has confirmed my conclusion.

The Death Penalty Information Center, a nonprofit that opposes capital punishment, claims that since 1979, 143 people who were convicted and sentenced to die were later proved innocent. This, of course, proves we have unjustly executed hundreds of innocents in the past.

There may be some who advocate some Faustian calculus that the execution of innocent individuals constitutes an unfortunate but necessary collateral damage to maintain a system that deters the murder of other innocent individuals. But that notion, in addition to being of questionable efficacy, is simply too far outside our shared national values to be acceptable.

So that leaves no justification for capital punishment other than our need for retribution. But the teachers from nearly every great faith tradition have been trying to wean us from this ancient reflex for some time now. And it is not like a sentence of life without parole is that lenient. Those serving life-without-parole sentences have the highest suicide rate among prison inmates. Can we not satiate our desire for retribution by taking away a person's freedom for life?

But here is the key point: A life sentence is reversible. Execution is not.

March 26, 2014

Erasing the Mark of Cain

I had been told he was a Baptist preacher and had worked as a prison chaplain in the Texas Department of Corrections for more than 30 years. When he walked into the restaurant in Huntsville to meet me for lunch, he fit the stereotype: Wavy hair combed straight back, western-style jacket and boots. When lunch was served, he asked that we bless our food.

But as he began to talk about the plight of prisoners and ex-offenders, he quickly shattered any preconceived stereotypes. For the next hour he spoke quietly but passionately about the desperate circumstances of individuals who had been released from prison, the inhumanity of the prison system, the apathy and cruelty of society and misguided public policies.

I was having lunch with Emmett Solomon because friends of mine had recently welcomed home a son from five years in the penitentiary. Their son's story is not unfamiliar. He developed a drug problem as a teenager that he was never able to whip. After four or five run-ins with our court system, he found himself in Huntsville.

It was an agonizing time for his parents, who were embarrassed their son had gotten into such serious trouble, petrified that he would be seriously harmed and haunted about what he might be enduring in prison. Any parent can imagine their relief when the call came that he was finally being paroled. Soon after the joyous homecoming, however, the reality began to sink in that the hardships were by no means over.

No one wanted to employ an ex-felon. No apartment complexes wanted to rent him an apartment. They learned that he was barred from scores of licenses. Forget getting any credit. My friends have made do, allowing their son to live at home and finding him a job in a family company. But as I watched them struggle with trying to help their son get back on his feet, I wondered what becomes of the vast majority of ex-offenders who have no such support systems.

For years at the TDC Emmett Solomon asked himself the same question and did not like the answer. So in 1993 he left TDC and formed the Restorative Justice Ministry Network. For the last 15 years, Emmett and his group have met men as they walked out of prison, welcoming them back to society and offering whatever help they can.

When people are released from TDC after serving their time, they are given $50 and a bus ticket home. Each day at 2 p.m., one or two buses leave Huntsville headed to Houston with 50 to 100 inmates released that day. It just so happened that Solomon and I were wrapping up our lunch at about 1:30 p.m.

"Would you like to go down and meet the guys being released today?"

Frankly, not what I had planned, but I agreed. When we arrived at the bus station, there was one unmarked bus, full of men, sitting with its engine idling. Solomon and his assistant, Bill Kleiberg, headed to the bus and motioned for me to follow.

I was not sure what to expect and have to admit a little apprehension about getting on a bus crowded with men just released from prison. I wondered if they would be belligerent because of the treatment they had endured or if there would be that sort of last-day-of-school air on the bus because their ordeal was finally over.

There was neither. The men sat quietly, waiting—obviously something to which they had become accustomed. Mostly they looked lost, staring into space or vacantly out a window. As I walked down the aisle shaking hands and chatting with those who would respond, I felt an overwhelming sense of despair and hopelessness from men just given back their freedom.

Suddenly, from the front of the bus, Kleiberg shouted, "My name is Bill. I am from the church and I am here to help you. I was released from TDC 12 years ago, just like you are being released today, and I am here to tell you there is hope." Instantly, the mood in the bus was transformed as the men eagerly snatched up the information packets Solomon's group had prepared on where they could find help in their home cities. The men suddenly became more animated, asking questions about the information we were handing them. I was amazed how deeply they seemed to appreciate even this small act of kindness.

At the rate we put people in prison in Texas, we need to be concerned about what happens when they are released. Worldwide, the incarceration rate is about 160 individuals for every 100,000 people. The second highest incarceration rate is Russia at about 650. The highest is the United States at 750. In Texas, the rate is about 1,000. That is, at any given time, about one person in 100 in Texas is in a prison or jail, six times higher than the world average and higher than even the world's worst dictatorships. Even if we stop putting people in prison at the current rates, we will be releasing 20,000 to 30,000 prisoners each year for many years to come just from TDC. Many thousands more will be released from county and city jails.

Most of those released do not have a family to take them in as my friends' son did. Solomon told me that only about 5 percent of the men released are met by family members. The odds are heavily stacked against those with no support system. With almost no chance of finding a job or a decent place to live, most fall back into trouble within a few years. TDC studies show that about one in three is back in prison within three years. If you extend the time frame to five years and include other prisons and jails, the recidivism rate is more likely 60 percent to 70 percent.

Since most of these inmates are also fathers, long absent from serving as any positive role model for their children, the cycle will likely be handed down to the next generation. The fact that Texas has one of the nation's highest incarceration rates and still has three cities with violent crime rates in the top 10 in the nation suggests that what we are doing now is not working.

In the Gospel of Luke, there is a story about a man whose son has come home after deserting his family. The father rejoices that his son, who was dead, is now alive. He was lost but now has been found. The truth is that we as a society would just as soon that these lost sons and daughters stay lost. We have branded them with the mark of Cain, made now more indelible with ubiquitous, easily searchable computer databases. Their crimes will never be forgotten. They will never be forgiven.

Driving back from Huntsville, I tried to imagine what it would be like to be coming home on that bus. To arrive at the Houston bus station with no one to welcome me, no one to offer any help and with nothing but $50 in my pocket. I tried to think what I would do if I were that person. I had no idea.

There are unquestionably many government policies that should be examined in the search for a solution to this dilemma. Many will be surprised to know that Texas is actually in the forefront of developing programs that attempt to prepare inmates for release. But there are no easy answers. Employers' and landlords' reluctance to employ or lease to ex-felons is hardly unreasonable, and given the potential liability issues, some would argue it's simply being prudent. Add that many ex-offenders, even if given a second chance, will disappoint us and it is easy to understand why society would just as soon wash its hands of these individuals.

There will be no solution until we as a society begin to feel differently about ex-offenders. People of faith should be in the forefront of such a transformation, for the principles of mercy and forgiveness are the cornerstones of virtually every great faith tradition. We can continue what we are doing now and likely get the same sad results, or perhaps we can find another way. I think a soft-spoken Baptist preacher from East Texas has, at least, pointed in the right direction.

November 8, 2009

Best Option for Ending Abortion

President Bill Clinton was apparently the first to suggest that abortion should be legal, safe and rare. As he so frequently did, Clinton summed up in a terse statement the consensus of Americans' feeling about abortion. But how legal, safe and rare is abortion today?

In the most recent data available, only 12 women died from complications from an abortion, compared with about 700 who die annually in childbirth. This undercuts those who support new restrictions on abortions because they want to make them safer.

Conversely, there does not appear to be much evidence to support the argument that more stringent abortion restrictions will make abortion more dangerous. In the year prior to the Supreme Court's handing down Roe v. Wade, only 36 deaths were reported from illegally performed abortions. It is possible, if not likely, this number was under-reported given the circumstances, but it still certainly suggests that claims by pro-choice advocates that thousands will be killed or injured in back-street, coat-hanger abortions is wildly exaggerated.

Some pro-choice advocates frequently cite World Health Organization statistics which show that about 47,000 women die annually worldwide from unsafe abortions as evidence of what could happen here if abortion is not readily available. However, the fatality rate from abortion correlates to the economic circumstances of the country, not the legal status of abortion. Bottom line is that abortions are very safe now, and greater restrictions seem unlikely to have much effect in either direction. All of the arguments to the contrary on both sides are mostly political theatrics.

The current legality of abortion turns on the circumstances of the individual case and the state in which the abortion would be performed, all of which is set against the backdrop of Roe v. Wade. In that landmark Supreme Court decision, justices basically weighed the right of the state to regulate abortion against a woman's right to control her own body. Grossly oversimplifying the ruling, the court's majority turned the issue on "viability" of the fetus, generally concluding a state has no right to regulate abortion in the first trimester. Layered on top of this general rule are those cases that involve special circumstances, such as rape.

There are now 41 states that have banned abortion after various intervals. The law Texas just passed prohibits an abortion after 20 weeks unless the health of the mother is at risk. So abortion is still legal in all states, although in increasingly narrower sets of circumstances. That the new Texas law set its outright ban at 20 weeks is another indication that this round of legislation is mostly for show because there are very few abortions performed after 20 weeks. According to data from the U.S. Centers for Disease Control and Prevention, fewer than 2 percent of all abortions occurred after 20 weeks, and many of those apparently have been for special medical circumstances that would be allowed under the new law regardless. So a 20-week ban is going to prevent very few abortions.

That brings us to the third goal, that abortion be rare. A threshold question with respect to the frequency of abortion is: What exactly constitutes an abortion? In particular, is the "morning-after pill" an abortion? It is important to understand that there are two different drugs that can be used after sex to prevent pregnancy. One is mifepristone, used in combination with other drugs, which causes the woman to expel a fully implanted and developing fetus. This procedure is commonly referred to as a "medical abortion" and is counted in federal data as an abortion.

However, there is another category of drugs, generally referred to as "emergency contraceptives," about which there is some disagreement. Most medical authorities believe that these drugs work primarily by delaying ovulation by the female and thereby preventing a union between the egg and a sperm. However, there has been some evidence to suggest that the drugs may also prevent a fertilized egg from implanting in the uterine wall and cause it to be discharged. There is considerable controverting medical opinion on this point, but if it is the case, pro-life purists who believe life begins at the moment an egg and sperm unite would consider it an abortion.

Whether "conception" has occurred when an egg is fertilized but fails to attach is an insoluble metaphysical question, but my guess is that most Americans do not believe the failure of a fertilized egg to attach to the uterine wall is the moral or medical equivalent to a person dying. In any event, I will stick with the definitions used by the CDC and exclude the emergency contraceptive drugs from considering how rare abortion is.

Through 2009 (the last statistics available) the U.S. Centers for Disease Control and Prevention estimates that 49 million abortions have been performed in the U.S. since Roe v. Wade. Today the total would exceed 50 million. To put that number in some perspective, the U.S. population would be 15 percent to 20 percent larger if all of those pregnancies had ended in live births.

The incidence of abortion increased rapidly in the early 1970s, even before Roe v. Wade. The number of abortions continued to escalate until 1990, when just over 1.4 million were performed. Fortunately, since 1990 that number has fallen by about half to 785,000 in 2009.

Perhaps even more startling has been the rate of abortions compared to the number of live births. This rate ran as high as 360 in the mid-1990s, meaning that about one in four pregnancies ended in an abortion in those years. That rate also has fallen since the mid-90s by about a third to 227 abortions for each live birth. Even so, today about one in five viable pregnancies ends in an abortion.

I do not know anyone who is in favor of abortion. I think the vast majority of Americans, whether they consider themselves for or against abortion rights, find 50 million abortions a troubling number and would want far fewer than one in five pregnancies to end in abortion. The question is: How do we accomplish that?

The stock answer for many abortion opponents is that we should intervene with the police power of the state and make abortions illegal. And if you believe that a person's life begins at conception, it is not illogical to also believe the state has a right to use its power to protect that life. The problem is that the exact point at which a new person is created is a metaphysical question, not a scientific one. There is no way to prove when a mass of cells becomes a person. As a result, there is a wide range of opinion on the matter. And the question becomes more muddied when you add special circumstances such as rape, incest or known birth defects.

It has been proved throughout history that a society cannot, over the long term, enforce criminal laws unless there is an overwhelming consensus that the conduct in question should be sanctioned. Prohibition, of course, is the quintessential example. And we as Americans have no overwhelming consensus on abortion. In fact, nearly a third of Americans do not even believe it is a moral question, much less one that would warrant criminal sanction.

Perhaps a better answer is suggested by looking at who has abortions and why. First, about 90 percent of women who have abortions list an unexpected/unwanted pregnancy as the reason. In other words, very few are for medical reasons.

Of course, women from every socioeconomic class have abortions, but overwhelmingly it is poor women who do. According to the Guttmacher Institute, nearly 70 percent of the women who have abortions make less than 200 percent of the federal poverty level (about $22,000 annually for a single woman). They are generally in their 20s and not married. African-Americans and Latinos have a disproportionate number of abortions, but they are also disproportionately represented in the lower income groups. A fact that I suspect will surprise most people: More than 60 percent already have a child.

The profile of women who have abortions strongly suggests that economic factors have a great influence. For a single mother in her 20s making less than $22,000 annually, the prospect of caring for and supporting another child must be daunting.

I have always found it ironic that my evangelical friends are normally among those most eager to make abortion illegal. I say ironic because there is no biblical or historical record of Jesus ever advocating changing any law. He lived in arguably one of the most immoral, corrupt governmental systems of all times. Yet he did not lobby Roman government to change its ways or seek to overthrow it. He sought to change hearts, not laws.

I have always thought that if those who so fiercely believe there should never be another abortion would spend a fraction of the time supporting young women faced with the dilemma of an unwanted pregnancy as they spend on trying make to them criminals, there would be far fewer abortions. Perhaps if young women facing that choice knew they could get health care, affordable day care so they could work, good schools where they did not have to worry about gangs and drugs, and faith or community groups that would help them, maybe—just maybe—they would decide not to end their pregnancy.

July 17 and July 20, 2013

Early Childhood Education

I t seems you can hardly pick up a newspaper or turn on a television news program without someone talking about the need for more early childhood education.

The discussion is being driven by a growing body of research showing that many children from underprivileged families start kindergarten behind their peers and that most never catch up. As a result, there has been much focus on how to create pre-kindergarten programs to try and offset this disadvantage.

We had a rancorous debate over a proposed ballot initiative in Harris County last year to impose a one-cent property tax increase to fund preschool programs. More recently, the amount of funding and the structure of such programs have become a major policy debate between our gubernatorial candidates.

For the most part, these programs focus on adding one year of some type of school before kindergarten. Whether it should a full day or a half, staffed by aides or professional teachers, run by private groups or the public school system are just a few of the questions being asked.

There are also a substantial number of critics of the programs who have parsed test results and concluded they have little actual impact on closing the achievement gap. And some early childhood specialists have argued that the age of 4 is too early to separate a child from her parent for the entire day.

Further muddying the waters, some research suggests that

stimulation, especially verbal, at even earlier ages be may be the critical factor.

Several studies have found that the more words a child hears starting at birth, the more successful he or she will be in school and may even score higher on IQ tests. Whether there is actually a causal connection is, of course, debatable.

But it seems to me what we are all really talking around is the fact that some kids have parents better able to give them a head start than do others.

While most parents demonstrate love for their children, there is nonetheless a range of parenting capabilities and dedication. A parent who cannot read obviously cannot read to his or her child. A single mother trying to hold down two jobs to make ends meet may not have the time to read to her child.

But even beyond educational or financial limitations, I wonder how many young parents are aware of how important reading to their child is. Or for that matter, when they should get their child a Social Security number, or what free preschool programs are available, or the importance of not drinking alcohol when you are pregnant?

I did not have my first child until I was almost 30 years old and remember feeling totally unprepared. I cannot imagine how the half-million teenagers now having babies each year must feel.

Statistically, more than 75 percent of our young people will go on to become parents. It is unquestionably the most important responsibility anyone will shoulder in life. And yet, just as we have no formal education to prepare young people to manage their finances, we have almost none to prepare them to be parents.

Why have we become so obsessed with teaching our children differential equations and the capitals of foreign countries but not ensuring that they have the basic life skills they are sure to need? And one cannot help but wonder if our high dropout rates do not have something to do with teaching a curriculum that many young people intuitively know will have limited relevance to their lives.

Don't get me wrong. This is not an argument against preschool programs. To the contrary, we must do everything we can to give these kids a chance to catch up, even if we cannot empirically measure the results. We can argue about methods and how to pay for it. We can refine the programs as we go. But doing nothing is not an option.

But if we focus only on the children without also trying to help the parents hone their parenting skills, I fear we may be pushing against a string.

It would seem obvious that any preschool program will be much more successful if the children's parents have some basic under-standing of early childhood development and what is at stake for their child.

April 9, 2014

Technology Renews Human Connection

O ver the past four weeks the world has been mesmerized by the unfolding events of the missing Malaysian Airlines Flight 370. There have been many aspects to the story, but most gripping has been seeing the anguish of passengers' families. People from every corner of the globe have cried and prayed and hoped beyond hope with those trapped in their interminable hell of not knowing what has happened to their loved ones.

It has mattered little that most of the families are Chinese, and many are Buddhist. Scores of countries have lent aid to the search effort, held prayer vigils and offered other assistance. Parents of every faith, nationality, creed and color have watched the parents of children who were passengers on the flight and readily understood their pain upon the loss of a child. A global community choked back tears when the husband of a flight attendant on the missing jetliner told the story of his 5-year-old daughter asking when her mother was coming home.

It is not that the tragedy of these 239 families is any greater than the thousands of others who lose loved ones to accidents or senseless diseases every day. The World Health Organization estimates that more than 3,000 people die each day just from injuries sustained in automobile accidents. The difference is that we have witnessed the Malaysian Airlines families' agony in high definition and real time.

The episode has reminded me of a photograph published a few

years ago by National Geographic of a grave that had been discovered in northern Africa. About 8,000 years ago, a young woman and two small children had been lovingly laid in the grave on a bed of flowers, holding hands and embracing each other.

Any human being in the world looking at that photograph knows that this family was likely buried by the missing family member, the husband and father. We do not know what language that man spoke, what god he worshipped or even the color of his skin. But across eight millennia and half a globe away, we all know intuitively the pain he felt in that tragic parting with his young family.

It is that ability to empathize with our fellow humans that separates us from other species. It is the foundation of civilization. But empathy is limited to our ability to experience the actual suffering of particular individuals.

Someone can tell us that 3,000 people died yesterday in car accidents, but unless we know the individuals or their families, it does not evoke an emotional response in us. Until the past several decades, our ability to share those tragic experiences with our fellow humans has been relatively limited to those nearby. And those from other parts of the globe or from different cultures seemed so remote and different from us that it was harder to imagine they shared our experiences and emotions.

But technology has changed all that. Now we can see the pain in the face of a Chinese factory worker who has lost his only child as easily as someone with a similar loss in our hometown. We can see the tears welling in his eyes, hear the trembling in his voice. Suddenly, he seems not much different from us.

This new ability to connect with other people from places far away and which most of us will never visit in person will change the world. Wars have largely been possible because of leaders' abilities to demonize their enemies. As people increasingly see that they have more in common with their fellow humans than differences, it will be harder to see them as enemies. If you have personally watched someone bury a child, it will be hard to ever hate that person.

Scientists have learned all humans share 99.9 percent of the same DNA, and some now believe that all humans are the descendants from a single woman who lived about 150,000 years ago, a "mito-chondrial" Eve. It is a great irony that while science and faith have supposedly been at war since the Enlightenment, science has now proved what every great faith tradition has been teaching for millennia: We are all brothers and sisters, literally.

And now with the revolution in communication technology, we are seeing for ourselves that it is true.

April 5, 2014

Dream of a Post-Racial America

About 20 years ago my oldest daughter, who was 10 at the time, and I were on our way to pick up a friend named Carol Jordan. Carol was a 5-foot-4-inch blond soccer mom with green eyes. On the way, my daughter asked me, "Dad, what is Carol's last name? I keep forgetting." I replied, "Jordan, like Michael Jordan. I think they may be cousins."

My daughter rolled her eyes (you dads out there know the eye roll I am talking about, the one your daughters reserve for you when you have said or done something they think is particularly idiotic) and said, "Dad, if they were cousins, I think Carol would be a little taller."

I could not help smiling, and feeling some pride, at the fact that when my 10-year-old daughter looked at a 5-foot-4-inch blonde and a 6-foot-9-inch African-American basketball star, the biggest difference she saw between the two was their height. I remember thinking to myself: Racism is dead in this country. The only question is: When are we going to have the funeral?

That was about 30 years after Martin Luther King Jr., gave his iconic "I Have a Dream" speech.

Another 20 years has passed, and I am still waiting for the funeral.

Not that there have not been seismic changes in the racial ethos of this country. If King were to be resurrected today, I think even he would be amazed to find that two African-Americans had served as secretary of state in Republican administrations and that an African-

American family now occupies the White House. And, of course, there are many other indications that we continue to move toward a post-racial America.

But in the last decade the progress toward King's dream seems to have stalled. I naively thought that the election of President Barack Obama would usher in that dream. Surely, if an African-American could be elected as the leader of the free world, we were past race. But in some ways it seems as though Obama's election has brought out latent racism in some quarters. I have a hard time believing that race is not at the core of some of most virulent hatred of the man you see so frequently in the blogosphere.

The left often leveled vitriolic, personal and often unfair attacks on George W. Bush. But I never heard anyone doubt his loyalty to the country or the fact that he was the Christian he professed to be, both of which have been repeatedly questioned in Obama's case.

And there are frequent reminders of how differently white and black Americans see some things. The George Zimmerman-Trayvon Martin incident last year and the trial of Zimmerman this year is one such instance. The vast majority of white Americans saw little or no racial implications while most black Americans did.

Watching the reaction to the verdict reminded me of a video I saw of two rooms reacting to the O.J. Simpson jury verdict years ago: one room of whites gasping in disbelief and the other a room of African-Americans cheering. No matter how much we wish it were not the case, white and black Americans still see the world very differently when it comes to many issues.

Rice University's Stephen Klineberg has tracked these differences over many years. Consistently, whites believe there is very little discrimination while blacks feel discrimination has only marginally receded. It is not that one perspective is right and the other is wrong. We are all products—indeed, to some extent, victims—of the environment in which we were raised.

And that brings me back to the conversation with my daughter in the car all those years ago. Because the polling shows clearly that young people care much less about race, and in fact are much less aware of it, than their elders.

Today, 10 percent of all marriages (over 5 million) are interracial. Something that was still illegal in many states when King gave his speech. And with millions of Americans having mixed heritage, the color line will be further blurred.

I have no doubt that King's dream of a colorblind society will be realized one day. Sadly though, I am beginning to feel that I will not see it in my lifetime.

Thomas Jefferson, writing near the end of his life about the abolition of slavery, said, "The revolution in public opinion which this cause requires is not to be expected in a day, or perhaps in an age; but time, which outlives all things, will outlive this evil also."

And so it will be.

August 28, 2013

Reflections of a Christian

For the last couple of years, I have taken pause at Christmas to think about my faith and its place in the world. This year it is hard to think about the current state of Christendom without taking note of the relatively unknown Argentinean priest who has become the leader of the Catholic church.

From all the controversy surrounding Jorge Mario Bergoglio this year, you would think he has been espousing some radical new theology. He has sent the conservative blogosphere/talk-show world into a tailspin with his frequent admonishments that we need to do more to help the poor. And social conservatives are apoplectic over his more conciliatory statements about social issues, especially homosexuality. But the truth is, Pope Francis is merely holding true to the core message of Jesus' Gospel. If Francis' ministry seems revolutionary, it is because so was Jesus'.

Religion is always co-opted by political and social movements. It is always a powerful argument to suggest that "God is on our side." And so it has been in our country's history. It may seem absurd today, but prior to the Civil War, many professing to be Christians quoted Scripture as justifying slavery. With the advent of atheistic communism in the 20th century, Christianity oddly got labeled as the religion of capitalism. While there are many Scriptures that praise and encourage industry, it was Jesus himself who told the rich young man to sell everything he had and give it to the poor. You don't get much more radical or anti-materialistic than that.

I was listening to a certain news channel a few days ago, and a right-wing commentator was railing about how Republicans were just as bad as Democrats, primarily for passing the budget compromise. What caught my attention was the way he couched his argument. He said, "The problem with the Republicans in Congress is that they have bought into this notion that we are our brother's keeper. We are not our brother's keeper, and Republicans need to stand up for that principle." That's a principle?

I have no idea what this person's faith tradition is, but he was presenting himself as a social conservative. Regardless, let me tell you, according to Jesus' teaching, we absolutely are our brother's keeper. In Matthew chapter 25, Jesus minces no words on how each of us will be judged. We will be judged on how we treat the hungry, the thirsty, the sick, the naked, the lonely and those in prison.

It is a sobering thought. If Jesus came back today would he recognize the United States as a country founded on his principles? Would he be marching in anti-abortion protests, trying to make them illegal or would he be ministering to young women with unwanted pregnancies to support them in keeping their babies? Would he be bashing homosexuals or instead showing them the same grace and love he showed an adulterer when he stood between her and an angry mob intent on stoning her? Would he be advocating that we make children criminals if they do not "self-deport" when they turn 18 years old?

How would he judge our treatment of the hungry, thirsty, sick, naked, lonely and imprisoned? I am afraid not too generously.

In Jesus' time, he was loved and hated. He was hated the most by the most religious in his society. The fact that Pope Francis evoked similar reaction is to his credit. Perhaps he can help all of us who profess to be Christians, Catholics and Protestants alike, to remember the true meaning of this season.

December 24, 2013

APPENDIX

Case Study of
Light Rail in Houston

*H*ouston, unlike many other large American cities, has been slow to embrace a rail transit system, although historically it has had a very good bus system. In 2003 the Houston voters approved a referendum on mass transit that included, among other elements, a nascent at-grade rail system as a trial.

After the referendum the pro-rail lobby seized on the referendum as a mandate to build an entire rail system, regardless of the costs or the limitations included in the referendum. The result is that a decade later, notwithstanding a rapidly growing population, Houston has fewer transit riders than in 2003, and our transit authority is virtually bankrupt.

As this train wreck unfolded, I wrote many columns highlighting the problems. I offer these in this appendix as a history of sorts of the issue for Houstonians. For others it is a cautionary tale of how community groupthink can trump facts and lead to a horrific policy outcome.

Six Myths About Light Rail

I n 1837, the great storyteller Hans Christian Andersen wrote the classic short story *The Emperor's New Clothes*. In the story a vain emperor is duped by two swindlers who convince him they can make him a magic suit of clothes that will be invisible to "anyone who was unfit for his office, or unusually stupid."

The emperor buys into the ruse and has the suit made. When it is finished, the emperor sees nothing but will not admit it because he fears others may be able to see the suit and thereby prove that he is unfit for his office. Soon his entire court is swept up in the self-deception as everyone claims to be able to see the nonexistent suit. Ultimately, the ruse is exposed when the emperor and his court go out for a public processional and a child in the crowd cries out that the emperor is naked.

For the last seven years, Houston's leadership has been engaged in exactly the same kind of groupthink about Metro's light rail plan. Anyone who has dared question this plan has been immediately relegated to the status of being unusually stupid, or at least some concrete-loving Luddite with a deviant desire for the automobile.

Well, at the risk of being deemed unusually stupid, I am here to say that Metro's light rail plan is naked as a jaybird. Here are six myths about Metro's light rail plan that you need to know. They demonstrate why we should scrap this plan and stop throwing good money after bad.

Myth No. 1: Metro's light rail will improve traffic congestion.
I am amazed at how often I hear that we must build Metro's light rail transit, or LRT, system to reduce traffic congestion. There is no study, projection or any other evidence that supports the proposition that the at-grade light rail system expansion that Metro is proposing will reduce traffic congestion. To the contrary, all the evidence predicts that it will make traffic substantially worse in the areas in which it is built.

To its credit, even Metro does not claim that its LRT will improve traffic congestion. Its own studies show significant operational degradation at every major intersection the LRT will cross.

Not that it takes a traffic engineer to figure out that an intersection like Post Oak and Westheimer is going to be negatively affected by adding two trains to what is already a nightmare crossroads. The idea that we are going to improve congestion by cramming a new transportation system into the same horizontal plane as existing vehicular traffic is nonsense on its face.

Myth No. 2: Houston will lose federal funds if it does not build Metro's light rail.
Actually, exactly the opposite is true. As a general proposition, the Federal Transportation Agency will pay for about 50 percent of the cost of a rail system. However, because Metro has included some segments that do not qualify for federal funds (primarily the Uptown line), the FTA will likely pay for only about 35 percent of the cost. That means that we will have to come up with about $2 of local money for every $1 of federal funds. However, for other kinds of transit improvements, like purchasing buses or improving the HOV system, Metro could qualify for as much as 80 percent reimbursement, thus leveraging our local dollars by as much as 4-to-1.

Myth No. 3: Metro's LRT will result in more transit riders.

As part of the federal application process, Metro was required to do studies of how much transit ridership will increase if the LRT is built. It is required to compare projected ridership for the LRT to a "no build" scenario, that is, to continue to rely on buses. What these studies show is that almost all the LRT ridership comes from people already riding a bus. Even the much-heralded Main Street line has resulted only in about a 20 percent increase in ridership over the bus lines serving the same corridor before it was built. If increasing transit ridership is the goal, which I believe it clearly should be, then there are much cheaper and more effective ways to do so.

Myth No. 4: Metro's LRT will reduce air pollution.

Again, there is absolutely no evidence that the LRT proposed by Metro will have any significant impact on air quality. Mostly, the LRT will be replacing some existing buses. Traffic studies show that it will result in very few cars coming off the road. While buses certainly are responsible for some emissions, those could be controlled at a much lower cost by converting to natural gas. And whether there is any overall reduction in emissions actually depends on what kind of fuel is used to generate the electricity for the LRT. If coal-fired electricity is used, the net result might be to increase emissions.

Myth No. 5: Metro can afford the LRT.

The cost of the LRT has exploded since it was first proposed in 2003. Then approximately 30 miles were to cost $1.2 billion, with the FTA expected to pick up half the cost. That is about $40 million per mile total cost, the local share being about $20 million per mile. Now the cost has soared to something well in excess of $3 billion, with the FTA contributing only about a billion. That works out to $100 million per mile total cost and a staggering increase in the local share to something over $67 million per mile.

In April 2008 Metro showed me its financial projections. At that time, Metro projected that the LRT would consume about 75 percent of its discretionary funds for the next 30 years. In fact, its projections showed that it would have only about $1.5 billion over the next 30 years to make additional improvements such as enhancing the HOV systems, building transit centers or adding commuter rail. But here is the kicker. That projection assumed a 5.15 percent increase in sales tax over the same period and a 7.5 percent annual increase in fares. Obviously, these projections are not working out so well, because Metro's sales tax revenue has plummeted and its attempt to raise fares has resulted in its largest ridership declines ever.

That is why you now are beginning to hear calls from Metro loyalists to end the general mobility payments to the city of Houston. However, with the city's finances running on fumes, that is unlikely to happen. The result is that Metro will either never be able to put the financing together for the LRT (and we will have wasted hundreds of millions planning it) or it will cobble together some highly leveraged plan that will permanently cripple Metro financially. In that case, the biggest losers in this will be Houston's transit-dependent citizens, because Metro will be forced to gut the bus system to pay for the LRT. Make no mistake; if the LRT is ever built, it will be done on the backs of the low-income working families that currently rely on the bus system to get them to and from work.

Myth No. 6: The voters approved Metro's LRT plan.
This may be the one that irks me most, because I was in the mix when the compromise plan that appeared on the 2003 referendum was struck. The 2003 referendum had three elements: (1) a $1.2 billion LRT system; (2) a roughly 50 percent increase in bus service; and (3) initiating a plan for commuter rail. Metro has completely abandoned

the bus expansion: We have fewer buses and bus riders today than we did in 2003. It also has done absolutely nothing to further the development of any commuter rail lines and has instead gotten in the way of other groups like Harris County when they have tried to initiate some action. The voters in 2003 did not approve just a light rail plan; they approved a comprehensive, multimodal system. Metro, for its own reasons, has abandoned what the voters approved in favor of its own grandiose vision.

Additionally, it should be noted that the voters specifically restricted Metro to borrowing $640 million to build the light rail system. Metro now plans to subvert that limitation by entering into a sale/lease-back arrangement with a separate subsidiary and actually borrow more than four times what the voters approved. Metro is always quick to invoke the moral authority of the 2003 referendum but casually ignores its inconvenient restrictions.

Most people who have heard of *The Emperor's New Clothes* think the tale ends with the crowd bursting into laughter after the child cries out and the emperor runs away embarrassed. But that is not how the story ends. Rather, the emperor shudders, fearing that the child is telling the truth, but nonetheless marches on with his courtiers trailing after him continuing to pretend to see his suit.

The question is whether we, as citizens and taxpayers, are going to demand that Metro live up to the 2003 referendum promising a multimodal transportation system that will address our ever-spiraling traffic congestion or whether we are going to allow Houston's courtiers to continue to march us toward a system that will financially cripple Metro, increase traffic congestion, gut any other transit initiatives for generations and destroy the bus system on which working families rely.

March 21, 2010

End of the Line

I come here not to praise Metro's light rail project but to bury it. Because the practical result of this week's Metro referendum to extend payments to the city of Houston, Harris County and Metro's other member cities is that finally, thank the Lord, this colossal boondoggle is dead. Metro will, of course, continue to pretend that the balance of the project can be built, but without the revenue stream that these payments represent, there is simply no money to continue to build the project. And for my part, good riddance.

There is an old saying that a camel is a horse designed by a committee. Metro's light rail project from the beginning was a transit camel instead of a horse. It was the result of political compromises and community groupthink rather than any hard transit analysis. Metro's own studies have consistently shown that this at-grade system would make traffic congestion worse everywhere it was built and make no meaningful contribution to improving air quality.

This was largely true because the studies have also projected it would only marginally increase transit ridership. For the most part, light rail systems do not attract new riders but instead merely move existing bus riders to the rail, and at an enormous cost. That certainly has been the experience with Houston's Main Street Line.

Metro likes to tout the Main Street Line's ridership with a claim that it carries more riders per mile than any light rail in the country. That statistic is obviously derived by dividing the number of riders by the length of the line. When the denominator, i.e., the length of the line, is a small number, the result is naturally going to be high. Guess what? Metro's Main Street Line is also one of the shortest in the country. So it is hardly surprising and totally meaningless that it carries more riders per mile than other lines.

The real measure of success should be how many new transit riders the Main Street Line has attracted compared to its cost. In 2007 I asked Metro how the ridership on the Main Street Line compared to the bus lines it replaced. At the time, there were about 28,000 boardings on the light rail system each day. Metro told me that was a 19 percent increase over the previous bus lines. In other words, Metro claimed that it had attracted about 6,000 new riders each day as a result of the rail line.

However, as of December 2011 the Main Street Line ridership had fallen to a little more than 25,000 daily riders, which is only a couple of thousand more than we had riding the buses in 2003. And of course this marginal increase has come at an enormous cost. Just the construction cost of the Main Street Line was about $400 million. That is a cost of about $200,000 per new rider, not even counting the ongoing operating costs. The riders would have probably appreciated it more if we had just bought them each a Bentley.

To be entirely fair, Metro is showing about a 6 percent increase in rail ridership this year, but still nothing that would justify the system's cost.

The good news is that now Metro hopefully will get back to focusing on improving the bus system on which so many in this city rely.

I have a friend who some years ago wrote a column for a newspaper in another city. A particularly controversial politician in that city had been one of his favorite subjects, providing fodder for many columns. My friend was truly devastated when the politician died unexpectedly from a heart attack.

I have to admit to similar mixed emotions about the demise of the light rail project. I am going to have to work much harder to find topics for this column now that I am not going to be able to beat this dead horse, or rather dead camel, any more.

November 7, 2012

What Do We Want?

In 2003, after many years of acrimonious debate over what role Metro should play in our region's transportation policy, we supposedly settled the issue with a referendum that was passed by a narrow margin. That referendum had three planks. First was a dramatic increase in Metro's bus service. Second was a financially limited commitment to build some light rail demonstration lines. Third was a commitment to begin the long-term planning for commuter rail to the suburbs.

Since 2003 Metro for the most part has abandoned the first and third parts of the plan. It has slashed the bus fleet by nearly a third and spent virtually no resources even thinking about commuter rail. It has, of course, been completely obsessed with the second part of the plan to build light rail and has far exceeded the financial limitations set out in the referendum and the cost estimates at that time.

Soon a decade will have passed since that referendum. During that time, taxpayers have pumped more than $3 billion into Metro. Its debt has increased fivefold, from about $250 million to $1.25 billion. Yet ridership for the past two years—about 81 million passengers annually—is the lowest since 1995 and down almost 20 percent just since 2006.

In 2013 Metro will be 50 years old. By that time taxpayers will have invested more than $12 billion in it. To put that in some perspective, those revenues could have been used to completely pay off the city of Houston's bond debt. Less than a third of that amount would have fully funded the city's pensions. Perhaps this is good time to ask exactly what we are expecting from our investment in Metro.

Metro has for many years had a mission statement. The current administration updated the mission statement in 2010 by setting out three strategic priorities:

- To provide first-class transit services including bus, rail, para-transit, vanpools, carpools, high-occupancy vehicle lanes and creative alternatives that are consistently safe, reliable and affordable.
- To build great transit infrastructure, including those projects voters approved in 2003, that are the foundation of an inte-grated mobility network.
- To earn the trust needed for Metro to be a welcome and effective partner in building the regional mobility network we need.

Metro's strategic priorities are so general they can mean virtually anything, which means they mean nothing. So instead of being guided by some overall policy objectives, Metro staggers from project to protect, initiative to initiative, buffeted by whatever political winds are blowing from City Hall or Washington, D.C.

I have been conducting my own informal poll about what people think is Metro's main job. Almost universally the response is to reduce traffic congestion. That is obviously a laudable goal and one that, if ac-complished, would have many benefits to our community. Of course, there is no evidence Metro has made any meaningful dent in conges-tion in the last 20 years, since its ridership has declined notwithstand-ing the sharp increase in the Metro service area's population.

What would Metro look like if its principal goal was to reduce traffic congestion? To start, it would not be investing billions in an at-grade rail system. A modicum of common sense should tell us that putting a new transportation system in the same horizontal plane that is already heavily congested is not a wise idea. And in fact, Metro's own studies show that at virtually every major intersection the light rail lines will cross, traffic congestion will get worse. Plus, who do you know who has been complaining about the terrible traffic jams on Harrisburg Boulevard or Main Street?

If the alleviation of traffic congestion was its real objective, Metro would be studying where it occurs most frequently and developing cost-effective remedies. The resources Metro devotes to this task are minuscule.

While I agree with the subjects of my informal polling that relieving traffic congestion should be a principal focus, there is another policy goal that is equally important. That is to provide reasonable transportation alternatives for those who cannot afford to own and operate an automobile.

There are, of course, many reasons why it is important to make transportation available to those who cannot afford a car, but the principal reason is to provide access to a job that can be the first rung on the ladder of economic advancement.

How would it change Metro if it adopted the dual mandates of relieving traffic congestion and providing the economically disadvantaged with some basic transportation? That is hard to say. But it certainly would not be slashing bus fleets and investing billions of dollars in rail lines in areas where there is no traffic congestion.

Perhaps before we invest another $20 billion to $30 billion of taxpayers' money in Metro over the next 50 years we should ask ourselves this basic question: What do we expect to get for that investment? What is Metro's *raison d'etre*?

March 21, 2012

Metro Does Something Right

There have been few harsher critics of Metropolitan Transit Authority over the last decade than yours truly. But there is one development at Metro that while overdue is certainly welcome: The recommendation by staff to begin the conversion of buses from diesel to compressed natural gas (CNG).

In the early 1990s Metro ran an unsuccessful pilot program with buses fueled by liquefied natural gas (LNG). At that time, natural gas engines were just regular diesel engines that had been slightly modified to run on natural gas. The performance was poor and the range limited. In addition, handling LNG at its extremely low temperatures has its own set of challenges.

So Metro decided that using natural gas to power buses was a bad idea. It was probably the right decision at the time, but Metro rigidly held on to that position for nearly two decades without any serious re-examination of the issue. In that interim, there were very significant advances in natural gas engine design as well as storage and drivetrain systems specifically designed to work with natural gas. As a result of the improved technology, much of the rest of the country began to make the switch to natural gas while Metro continued to turn its back on it. By 2011 about 30 percent of all new transit buses were built to be powered by natural gas.

Fortunately, the new board appointed in 2010 by Mayor Annise Parker made an early commitment to take another look at natural gas. That commitment got sidetracked with all the problems the board inherited (and a few it created itself) over their first couple of years on the job. But, better late than never, the report on the staff findings from its study was finally presented to the Metro board last year.

It found what other fleet operators have been finding for some time now: Natural gas is considerably cheaper than diesel. It burns cleaner, resulting in fewer emissions (about a third fewer carbon emissions). The cleaner burn also results in less buildup in the engine and therefore lower maintenance costs. There are some higher upfront capital costs. Natural gas buses are more expensive, although that difference is rapidly coming down. Also, refueling stations must be constructed; they are not cheap. But some natural gas suppliers will build the stations in exchange for long-term supply contracts. When all the factors are weighed, the Metro staff concluded that CNG clearly had the edge.

Accordingly, Metro staff recommended that the agency begin purchasing CNG buses in 2014 and gradually work ultimately toward an all-CNG fleet. The board has not yet acted on the recommendation, but Metro officials told me recently that they expect to shortly have a request for proposals for the board to consider. Based on the board's public comments and some conversations I have had with individual members, the staff's recommendation seems likely to win board approval.

I wish it had not taken this long to get here, and frankly it would be nice to see a little more aggressive implementation schedule than the Metro staff is currently contemplating. But for an organization that was dead-set against natural gas just a couple of years ago, this is real progress.

Now maybe the city, county and other government agencies in the region will follow Metro's lead and begin exploring opportunities to switch their fleets to natural gas. After all, Houston is arguably the natural gas capital of the world. Should we not be the first to embrace and herald its advantages?

May 18, 2013

Acknowledgments

There are a number of people I would like to thank for their help on this book. First and foremost is Jeff Cohen, the Executive Editor of the Houston Chronicle's Editorial pages. Without his early encouragement and constant coaching and editing I would never have found my writing voice in the first place, nor would I have sustained the effort. Notwithstanding that he continues to be confused about light rail in Houston, he has been a great friend, mentor and above all, a great editor.

I would also like to recognize and acknowledge the contribution of my parents. Their admonishments about education were of course key. But more important was their compassion for their fellow human beings and strong social conscience, which were the prisms through which they viewed the world and settled on their opinions about issues. In their case it was a by-product of the Christian faith. Their core beliefs have been a great legacy to me.

I want to thank the thousands of readers who have written to me. Whether they agreed or disagreed, I almost always found their input interesting. Quite often their views ended up informing my own. I also want to thank them for the numerous ideas for columns they gave me. Their energy and passion about these topics fed my own and helped me keep making those deadlines.

Finally, I want to thank Fritz Lanham for devoting the time I did not have to pull this material together and help in his gentle way to discern between "good" columns and those which were "less good."